The Anointi
The Anointin

ẞ

Copyright by: Parice Parker

Copyright Library of Congress: TXu1-287-817

ISBN 09787162-1-3

Author: Parice Parker

Cover Imagine & Illustrations: Parice Parker

Chief Editor: Shanekia Bryant

Editors: Mrs "G" & Carolyn Wise

Printed In The United States of America

Fountain of Life Publisher's House

www.booksfolph.com

The Anointing Power of Your Hands

If You Want It, Then Lay Your Hands On It. "Let The Anointing Destroy Your Yokes & Cause Your Vision To Speak"

Chapters

Introduction   ii.

Part One: Press And Push   *1*

Part Two: Fighting the Battle - Defeating Your Giant   1(

Part Three: The Heart of Your Hands Beating At Work   37

Part Four: Spiritual Inflammation   59

Part Five: Your Heart Intent   8(

Part Six: Praying To The Point Of No Return   96

Part Seven: Seven Keys To Embrace The Anointing   12(

Part Eight: Getting To Know Your Hands Personality   13ξ

Part Nine: Oops My Hands Fell Into Sin   15ξ

Part Ten: Finger Out Your Faith   17(

Special Dedications   198

The Anointing Powers Of Your Hands

Introduction:

The strength God will bestow on your life by lifting your hands. It will be overfilled with His Anointing. Absolutely nothing in this world could exist. No vision could have ever flourished without one laying his or her hands upon it. Whatever, you are planning to accomplish it shall be done in the name of JESUS. You must exercise your faith daily, for you to strengthen supernaturally. It all depends on your faith in Him. He wants you to have the best of everything in life. When one tries with all their heart through the powers of God, they are never forsaken. God's word is His promise, so if you stand on His word, His promises will be fulfilled in your life. He promises us, a prosperous life, good health, conquering power, wealth, fulfillment, peace, joy, happiness and so on. Believe me, God did not create you to do without! Absolutely not, God said, "The Anointing Powers are in your hands, use them

The Anointing Powers Of Your Hands

to His fullness." God wants you to lay your hands on the vision He has given you. By your faith, your vision shall speak, because faith without works are dead. Lay your hands on it and watch Him work in them. Let God Anoint the works of your hands; just lay your hands on it.

The Anointing Powers Of Your Hands

Part One

Press & Push

"As You Press & Push You Will Soon Overcome."

The Anointing Powers Of Your Hands

Once you begin to desire The Anointing to flow through the tips of your fingers you will do all that is necessary to receive it. It is time to make room for The Anointing to move into your life. You will not allow any sort of excuse to accompany your mind. When you hear

receive instructions when God speaks. As we receive those instructions, our freedom is released as we follow through with them. However, your press is not going to be easy neither is it going to be smooth sailing. Philippians 3:14 says, I press toward the mark for the prize of the high calling of God in Christ Jesus. If you really want The Anointing Powers to work through you, then you are going to have to do something out of your ordinary state of mind. You will not be able to do the ordinary with the work of your hands, so now it is time for the extraordinary to speak through you. **Prove your point to God, do what you need to receive The Anointing.** *Allow the Anointing to feel the unusual effort of your press. Let the Anointing feel the heart of your press until The Anointing move in your life.*

The Anointing Powers Of Your Hands

*If you want it, then you must put your hands on it like you have lost your mind. Place them in a position to move forward and see God work through them. God is ready to birth a Fresh Anointing out of you. Just as the woman with the issue of blood that suffered for many of years and in many ways, she pressed her way out. This woman realized that if Jesus had all the power many said He had, then she was not prepared to suffer any longer. No one knew what this woman was feeling, the pain and agony. When we think of issues we blow it off as soon as we think about it, but issues are extremely painful. Actually most people cannot handle the amount of pain these issues will cause. Many will just simply give up. However, this woman refused to give into her issues. She struggled to the point of no return. Her mind was made up to reach Him. **Stretch your faith and trust God more, let your faith move your mountains.** This woman was not prepared to allow any sort of issues neither blood to stop her from stretching her faith. In many case's, we all have begun to stretch for Jesus and many things have tried to interrupt our stretching effort. Just because things look dim in your life, do not give up. Though many obstacles get in your way, keep on* stretching until God bring you out. **Often many live in a zone of comfort with their faith, until their faith cannot cause them to be moved.**

This woman was full of issue's, the bible did not list them all. So many, until it caused trouble and agony to become the way many identified her. Issues was her first description and blood was her last – The Woman with The Issues of Blood. Many did not expect Jesus to bring this woman out, but He did. Her issues were countless, but she did not let them stop her from reaching for Jesus. Once she reached for Him she wanted to touch the Extraordinary Supernatural and she did. She struggled to press and many obstacles she had to press through. You cannot even begin to be broken through until you begin to press. In order to press and push you must be positioned to make a move. Your pushing effort must be extraordinary and you will not allow anything or anyone to stop you. The only thing that should be on your mind is coming out. I do not know all that you are going through, but I know that Jesus has the power to bring you out. Though many things may try to get in your way, you must

The Anointing Powers Of Your Hands

push and press at the point of no return just push your way out. I consider this a Supernatural Birthing. Once you feel the Supernatural move on you, then you will expect the extraordinary things to come forth in your life. The truth is that your reality to your dreams are in your press. I know as I had journeyed in my high calling many things tried to hinder me and the enemy had purposed to stop me.

*Everything in my life grew to a state of oppression in every way. When I tried to put one foot forward, something else happened, to hold me back. Often times my visions tarried and sometimes **I did not have everything I wanted to get through one threshold to another, but I had my faith.** I simply used the voice of the Lord to keep me in a pressing state. Though you may think that you do not have everything you need, you have more than enough to make it through. Regardless, do not allow a need to stop you. As you will continue your press, God will bring you out. Just continue to move forward. Push and press your way through. You must move and be prepared to move forward in a pressing position with no pushing tolerance level. It is time that your ordinary*

The Anointing Powers Of Your Hands

pressing state of mind becomes the champions of weight lifters. Every time I suffered, The Anointing increased my faith. **When I was spiritually disturbed, The Holy Ghost was my counselor. Oh what a wonderful Counselor He is.** When my enemies bombed rushed me, Jehovah Jireh was my provider. However, when I called out to Jesus the enemies lost their battle. This press is getting ready to be the most potent press of your life. It is going to break you completely free, from everything that has tried to hinder the works of your hands. In addition, when this press is over the results are going to be extremely effective within your life. All of your enemies will be destroyed and all your troubles will be over as your latter will be far greater than your beginning. Get ready to push and press, until The Anointing cause your enemies to be incompetent. I pushed my way because I wanted my prize. Getting to your prize is through your press and you are going to need The Supernatural Pressing Power Pushing through you. You have to get to the mark, then your prize will be waiting there for you. Everything that God has marked in your life will be available as you press; He has a mighty way of causing us to press our way out. We all have a certain *mark in our life that God predestined us to reach.* **While your mother was in her mother's womb God had already predestined this press to come out of you.** *Your mark is your unlimited resource to heaven that will be available for you to get your prize. Press your way through as the woman with the issue's of blood. In addition, that was her last press she ever had to endeavor, it delivered her out of a life full of agonizing issues. Surely, if The Anointing delivered her then The Anointing has the power to deliver you too.*

It is just like being a baby in a mother's womb, when that baby is developed and ready to come out it will press its way out of the womb. Even though that child is entering a world that is strange, it does not care the baby just wants out. Regardless of the time of day, the occasion or the doctors reports that baby is coming when it is ready to come out and nothing or no one will stop it. So therefore, whenever you are truly ready to come out, you will press and push, until the Anointing Powers of Your Hands will cause you to be delivered. Let the Anointing work through you, just lay your hands on it and watch what God is going to do for you.

There was a man known by the name of Doubting Thomas and he too had to learn to stretch his hands forth. Isaiah 58:9 says, Then shalt thou call, and he shall say, answer; thou shall cry, and he shall say, here I am. If thou take away from the midst of thee the yoke, the putting forth of the finger, and speaking vanity. Thomas did not trust his friend's word or his own eyesight. Thomas realized that his doubt was a yoke that needed to be removed. Many times people will trust the things they can hear or see, but God wants our trust in the unseen and the things that have not happened yet. I have learned through the years that the eye's can fool you. I once went into a business deal trusting my eyes as my hopes were lifted. I thought this deal was perfect, but it was not. Everything your eyes see is not all that it appears to be. We must be careful of the things we allow our eyes to see and ears to hear - research more until Jesus give you clarity. There were times that Thomas needed to call on the Lord, but he doubted Him because he was unsure of his faith. His doubt caused him to be unfaithful to God and continuously made him feel insecure. You must let God know that you truly trust Him. God wants us to trust Him in our best and worst times in life. I know when I have gotten in messed up situations, God always brought me out. In the beginning, I did not trust Him as I should, but the more I cried out to Him is the more I grew to trust Him. God knows everything about us. He knows exactly what you are going to have to go through, even before you go through it. Your trials and tribulations will bring you closer to God, just as the woman with the issue's of blood. If it had not been for her many agonizing issues, then how could she have ever pressed her way into The Anointing? God wants you to reach for Him, until you touch The Anointing. He wants you to press harder towards Him until you feel His presence move through you. The Anointing flowed through her fingertips and removed all her issues. In addition, He always knows how to gain our trust.

Occasionally, we have allowed our voices not to be heard by God all because of a little doubt. I have found to believe that if you do not believe in

The Anointing Powers Of Your Hands

*whatever it is that you want to accomplish, then no one else will. Out of the many things I desired to achieve, many did not believe that I could and often times doubt tried to steal my belief. Moreover, I continued to try my best to trust in the Lord. God wants you to believe even when it seemed though things are not working out. Your way out is determined up to your belief and your amount of trust in Him. If you have the faith a size of a mustard seed, surely God will remove your mountains. Most of these are due to the fact most people's faith is in a paralytic state and that will cause conflict of movement. When you are in a paralytic state regardless of what you want to do or try, you simply will just need a miracle. Paralytic faith will stop your hands from plunging forth into the depths of Jesus. Doubt will stop you from being filled with The Anointing and it will cause you not to press and push. It will be impossible to move forward or just move at all. **I tell many do not let the yokes destroy you but allow the powers of God to destroy your yokes.** John 20:27 says, Then saith he to Thomas, Reach hither thy finger, and behold my hands; and reach hither thy hand, and thrust it into my side: and be not faithless, but believing.*

The Anointing Powers Of Your Hands

Thomas moved forward though his yokes of fear and doubt tried to stop him. The Anointing begin to remove his yokes of insecurities once he reached for Jesus. When Thomas touched Jesus wounds it gave him an incorruptible faith. No man would ever have to convince him again because he touched The Truth for himself. Moreover, after Thomas put his fingers through the wounds of Jesus he said, "My Lord and My God and then Jesus spoke to Thomas and said, " Blessed are those that have not seen but believe". At this point, a mustard seed of faith begins to grow in Thomas, until his faith had no more room for doubt.

Jesus wants us to believe before we receive our blessings. Often times, our level of belief is not at the height to cause the level of blessings to be poured into our lives. God wants our trust just because He is God. He wants us to know that He has the power to make things happen, before He made things appear in our lives. Trust in the unseen, believe in the impossible and prove your trust more to Him by believing greater in Him. God wants

The Anointing Powers Of Your Hands

you to trust Him like never before. He wants you to believe in The Anointing. It is All- Powerful and it releases your miracles. God has allowed your dreams to be big. He has given you vision and trusted you with it. God wants you to trust Him for it. Put your hands on it and let God work in you. How is it that God is God, if He does not show us in action? God is powerful and He loves to anoint our well doings. He gains more recognition of how powerful He is, when He works a miracle in your life. He wants your hands on it, the proof has been written but where is your belief? God wants your belief manifested in Him so that others can see just how powerful He really is. He wants to manifest victory in your life. Let The Anointing take control of you. It will lead you into a life of pure satisfaction. I guarantee that your life will obtain greater worth as He will obtain greater glory through the works of your hands. Many will then say, it only had to be God to cause such a miraculous thing to happen in your life. John 20:28 says, And Thomas answered and said unto him, My Lord and my God.

The Anointing Powers Of Your Hands

You do not know the half of what God will do in your life. He will fix every broken down thing in your life, repair every damage structure, heal every sickness and lead you into a life full of prosperity. His Anointing will prosper you, as it will set you free. I know that every part of your hand has a serving purpose and it's to serve Him Glory. If we never use what God has given us, then how is He going to be recognized as God in our life? All you have to do is reach for Him. Once Thomas felt His presence, He claimed Jesus to be His God and His Lord. When you truly know God, you will praise Him for everything in your life including over the work of your hands. However, that is why the work that God has given you must be complete. Surely, you are ready to gain. The question is; are you willing to do everything for your dreams to come true.

A bricklayer cannot lay one brick without the other until he or she reaches forth with his or her own hands, to grasp the next brick. Then that particular brick that you are grasping must be placed into perfect position, just hold on to it. The Anointing Power is

The Anointing Powers Of Your Hands

*in your reach; to receive it you must lift your hands. In addition, there is grasping power and it lies within the palms of your hands. If you pick up something heavy, with your fingertips – it will be hard to hold onto. So therefore, you need to place it within the palm of your hands. Your palm serves a holding purpose and your strength lies within it. It is the part between your fingers and your wrist. It is your holding power. **Just remember in order for you to move forward you must place one foot in front of another**. When you make one step, God makes two. Proverbs 3:27 says, Withhold not good from them to whom it is due, when it is in the power of thine hands. You must begin to step out on faith to settle into your promises. God wants you to reach your dreams, that is why He has given you the vision. Once you reach your dreams, then you will begin to live the life you desire. He shows us things in many different forms to inspire us to move forward in our life. He will let you see what your life could be, if you obey Him. He is the one that has caused your heart to desire this vision, which is why you cannot get it out of your mind. He expects you to believe in Him. In addition, He wants you to lay your hands on it. Hold on to your prom-*

*ises and move forward until you reach your promise land. Every want and heart desire is there, waiting on you. God wants you to use the power He has given you. The Anointing Powers that are in your hands are designed to get you to your land. A land full of promises to bring your heart desires to reality. God wants you to reach for higher. It is a blessing to have big desires and to be able to visualize them. It is a privilege and a gift from God because everyone does not have vision. Matthew 13:17 says, For verily I say unto you, That many prophets and righteous men have desired to see those things which ye see, and have not seen them; and to hear those things which ye hear, and have not heard them. **Dreams are dreams but visions speak boldly.** You are a special person to God and He wants to instruct you on how to accomplish your vision. He wants you to reach the top and He created you to be more than a conquer. It is going to be a day to rejoice when your vision speaks boldly to the world that He is All-Powerful. Know that God will grant your heart desires soon after you lay your hands on it. The Anointing powers are in your hands. Once you lay your hands on it, God will turn your negatives into positives.*

Part Two

Fighting the Battle

Defeating Your Giant

"The battle is not yours, it is the Lords."

The Anointing Powers Of Your Hands

You should not fear any situation because God does not produce fear. When you conclude in your mind that faith is dead without works, then you will begin to exercise your faith – stretching it to the point of no return. 11 Timothy 1:7 says, For God has not given us the spirit of fear; but of power, of love, and of a sound mind. Fearing life is not of God. Grow up into a David spirit, not allowing a huge giant that is bigger than you to destroy your hope, peace, joy or steal your life promises. **Too many have given into fear and never made it to their promise land.** God wants his children hearts to be noticed, through the way we live, the things we do and through the things that we encounter. You can either become to be a slave to your giants or you can be a powerful champion in the name Jesus. If we continue to walk in fear, then how is it that we are going to show others, that God is real? God takes great pleasure in our victories. He is awarded the Glory and then you are awarded the honor. Though we feel the force of the many difficulties that has surfaced in our lives, it does not mean that we should not face them.

The Anointing Powers Of Your Hands

Facing your giant will end all fears within this area of spiritual growth. Just as the rest of the Israelites, surely, David could have feared but instead as a young boy, David had more courage than the ones that ruled in the army. As David prepared to fight the giant, he proved that he had more courage than King Saul. 1 Samuel 17:42 says, And when the Philistine looked about and saw David, he disdained him; for he was but a youth, and ruddy, and of fair countenance.

David was not thinking about the gigantic size of Goliath, because his heart was set on the size of his faith he had in God. David's faith was recognized as a child, and his belief was beyond words. He had the faith like no other and his faith astonished the heart of God. He did not have time to fear because his faith was strong. Regardless, the size of the whole army, David saw that they were incapable of defeating this giant. As David look towards the army, he could not find one that was prepared to challenge Goliath. David heard the voice of the giant, but his voice still could not compare to his God. David asked the soldiers that were afraid of Goliath, "Who is he to challenge the armies of the living God?" David had the courage because he was a Faith Walker. He had the armies of the living God fighting through Him. Psalms 27:14 says, Wait on the Lord: be of good courage, and he shall strengthen thine heart: wait, I say, on the Lord.

Your strength is in Him. David was one to know of God's mighty strength. He had experienced fighting many battles. I too had this one giant fighting me. We had a lot of trouble from this building. Oh, it was awful. The roof leaked, we needed flooring, electrical repairs and walls. You name it we needed it. We put a lot of time and effort in this building. Actually, we needed a new building, though at times, we must be tested. Sometimes God wants to see how you are going to handle yourself in certain battles. Our ministry survived many battles as we persevered, we made it. We continued paying the expenses as we repaired the building. This building was our giant. No matter how hard things was we never gave up. God test our hearts and you never know when He is going to test you. The key to passing the tests are that you must be good to everyone, regardless. Showing love is the key. So there-

fore, I believed the entire test through dealing with this experience, we passed. The more effort we put in this building the rougher things got. We had to learn true struggle and then how to give in to the power of God. As we fought, the giant fought back. Our hearts was changed after many experiences took place to cause us to develop spiritually. The more mountains we climbed through faith is the greater some of us grew, while others could not hold on any longer. Genesis 22:17 says, That in blessings I will bless thee, and in multiplying I will multiply thee as the stars of the heaven, and as the sand which is upon the sea shore; and thy seed shall possess the gate of his enemies.

Sometimes people just need a break in order for God to bring them through. You never know when God is going to use you to help break someone else free. So many told me I am going to help you. Others said God sent me to help you. Then another, you are the one God said for me to help. They all just talked, but no action. Some even attempted to help, but their eyes could not stay focused on the powers of God. Imagine if every superstar right now would have not met the one person that God worked through, to bless him or her. Think of how many people overlooked someone and as they made it, they wished they had helped. I just left it in the hands of God as I prayed God to bless their hearts to love more earnestly. Selfishness, is not of God. It is something how people will have what you need but are not willing to help or give. I have had friends that saw my need but walked out too. Nevertheless, members that were not willing because of their busy schedules. I laughed as I cried and prayed, as I was hurt. Often many souls will suffer because of someone else's greed. I always said, "When God bless me out I will not treat people as many have treated me." Matthew 5:44 says, But I say unto you, Love your enemies, bless them that curse you, do good to them that hate you, and pray for them which despitefully use you, and persecute you. It is so much better to give than to receive. David was one that was willing to fight this giant and so was I. Allow no giant to threaten you and know that God is fighting your battles. Do not be bothered when people do not stick to what God told them to do for you. Walk on in your faith. Though things are not happening, as you want them to they will. God is working your situation out. Remember everything happens for a purpose and God will reveal to you the reason.

I begin to put my hands on what God had given me. He wanted me to use what I had to continue ministering. Eventually the worth of the building became worthless, God gave us greater vision. God knows how to remove the giants out of your life. I use the gifts He had given me and I ministered in song and in books. Psalms 86:13 says, For great is thy mercy toward me: and thou hast delivered my soul from the lowest hell. God taught me through this one experience, to wait on Him. He expanded my vision and caused me to be more of a Faith Walker. Just take note of how much God is going to bless you, because your heart was positioned to be a blessing. Live this and you will be blessed forever.Genesis 22:17 says, That in blessings I will bless thee, and in multiplying I will multiply thee as the stars of the heaven, and as the sand which is upon the sea shore; and thy seed shall possess the gate of his enemies. I believe that many forget how they achieved and advanced in life. Upon every time when someone makes it – it is always due to someone else *helping him or her. Whether they were noticed or someone gave them a chance, perhaps their work or talent interest someone to invest in them. As you make it, remember where you come from and be prepared to help someone else achieve. I have prayed for years that God would continue my heart to love more and help others. God simply wants us to bless others that are less fortunate. Want peace in your life and to follow what is in your heart. Be prepared for your giants to cease. Realize that in the putting on of your hands that you serve a living God that has all power. Do not allow any one to miss-treat you and make you feel like you are beneath him or her. We must conclude that anyone serving a living God should be treated with love and respect. Sometimes God will try you by your heart. Keep your heart clean and pure with God always. Do not allow any giant in your life to make you appear less. We serve a God that deserves respect always. He judges us on how we treat one another. David loved God too much to allow a giant to over power the God that lived in him. God is powerful and He deserves better than most people give Him. During your battles, your life will show whose in control. Can you relate to how David felt,*

The Anointing Powers Of Your Hands

who does that giant think he is compared to my God? We serve a living God with all power. As we stand up to our many giants, God will give us greater wisdom and vision. Through your courage, you will gain more strength as you continue to stand. God will also flourish your vision. Again, man looks on the outer, but God knows what is on the inside of you. David was one that gave God great respect during his battle with the giant. We must look at the giant and say, "Who is he to challenge the armies of the living God?" He was a mighty blessing to his army as he defeated Goliath. Not only did he win, but look at all the souls that were saved because he was a Faith Walker. The more you defeat your giants are the more your children will posses the gates of their enemies. Your victories will cause you to testify and the more strength in Him you will gain. You must continue in your faith, many will be delivered from their giants as you continue. Fight with an expectancy to win. However, you will be bruised and wounded but fight to the end. Use your faith to anoint your situation. Allow your faith to move God, so therefore you will not have to work so hard. I was stripped in many battles to man but, God clothed me in His Armour. Just as

The Anointing Powers Of Your Hands

David I could not live by the things my eyes saw, I lived by faith. If faith were not so, I would have died. Faith has caused many to survive. With faith, you will have the victory at all times. 11 Timothy 1:7 says, For God hath not given us the spirit of fear; but of power, and of love, and of a sound mind.

Your battles are to strengthen you and to spiritually develop you. Help others in the time of their needs. Bless others as God has blessed you. Let others see the power of God in you and show them the power of love. Let your heart be prepared to help others with the love of God beating in your heart. God does not intend you to be fearful in any situation. When you are His, there are no incidents or accidents. God knows how to make things happen in your life. However, we make many mistakes but God makes absolutely none. As He put His claims on you, everything that has happened in your life was meant to be. Some are to strengthen you, while others will make you wiser and give you courage. This battle will bring you closer to His light. In addition, it will awaken you more. As David was preparing to battle he was also preparing to win. He knew God was more powerful than Goliath and before he fought, he knew the battle was already won. Know that you are a winner because God is fighting your battles, as The Anointing will be in you.

When you are in the hands of God where does fear fit in? The power of The Anointed is awesome in works. Hebrew 10:31 says, It is a fearful thing to fall into the hands of the living God. He will permanently remove any giant out of your life, without question. Only the Powers of God can beat your giants down. David knew that he was in the hand of his living God, so fear could not enter his heart. A giant to David was not a threat or any other detail. David looked at Goliath as nothing compared to his God. He kept in mind the power of the living God he served. I know something miraculous has occurred in your life. You knew it was only God. Just like me, I had to experience falling into the hands of God. That giant could not make me fret because God made me move. Proverbs 8:22 says, The LORD possessed me in the beginning of his way, before his works of old. One time or another you *have conquered something bigger than you in your life and only God was able to receive that glory. You knew within your heart that it was not you, but it was because of the powers of God. He rose up your hope. That is the exact hope that you need right now in order to gain the victory of winning this battle. David remembered his previous victories that he had won. When he killed the lion and smote the bear with the anointing power that was in his hands. David admired the powers that God had placed within his hands. He knew it was all through the anointing. He knew it was the powers of his living God, fighting through him. Proverbs 3:26 says, For the LORD shall be thy confidence, and shall keep thy foot from being taken.*

Perhaps you are in a LOSING STATE IN YOUR LIFE THROUGH YOUR BATTLES. In addition, your giants are defeating you. REMEMBER THAT IT CAN ALL CHANGE THROUGH YOUR FAITH. I know that the power of God can turn it around for you. Though your battle seems impossible, know that God has given your hands the power. ***People fail in life due to their negligence in listening to God.*** *Nevertheless, we can hear Him,* *but the question is do we listen. God wants your heart, mind, body and soul to be pure well as your hands to be cleansed. Eventually it all will work out even though the enemy wants it to work out for his benefit. Always believe that God can use and change every heart. He surely changed me. Know that you are in His hands always. JEHOVAH will take care of you just as He took care of David. Not only will He take good care of you, He will cover all that is around you. When He took care of David, God also covered the Israelites. That is why it is so valuable to be amongst the people that are covered by the hands of God, it will save your life. God has the power to cover a whole army, so what are you worried about? Deuteronomy 33:3 says, Yea, he loved the people; all His saints are in thy hand; and they sat down at thy feet; everyone shall receive of thy words.*

Whenever God is in full control, then what is it to fear? You must realize that you are in the hands of the Almighty. You should never fear because God is working in your life. While you are in God's hand, then fear should not be an obstacle. God has all power in His hands and since He is your covering then know you are going to win this battle. Know that you are setting in the palm of His hands and by any means, nothing can or no one will hurt you? Do not allow fear to stop the Anointing to move over the works of your hands. Matthew 11:29 says, Take my yoke upon you, and learn of me; for I am meek and lowly in heart: and ye shall find rest.

Once you begin to place the yokes of Jesus around your neck, then you will begin to grow in the power of God. *You will gain the anointing power that will loose many to freedom. You will be very compassionate, never looking at any mans down fall. You will begin to pray for them and your heart will feel love that it has never felt. Your spirit will become meek and humble because now you will begin to understand Christianity. You will know its purpose and definition is love. You will walk by faith and be considered by many to be a Faith Walker. II Corinthians 5:7 says, (For we walk by faith, not by sight:) Regardless of where it is many will not only see that you are a peculiar person, but they will feel The Anointing as you speak, walk, move and pray. You will not need to be* *introduced, because The Spirit of Jesus will be in you. As they look on you, they will receive power just by seeing your faith. Jesus is telling you to take His yoke, learn of Him. He wants you to come on your own free will and get it. Though you must suffer as Jesus did, go through as He did you will also rise up as He did. Surely many wants to reach the mountaintop, but very few would care to climb the mountain for themselves. Do not allow the enemy to operate with smoothness in your life. Proverbs 8:35 says, For whoso findeth me findeth life and shall obtain favour of the Lord. The word of God instructs that the spirit knows the spirit by the spirit. Jesus has a powerful spirit that frightens the enemies away. His spirit is unique; it has healed the blind, caused the lame to walk, given many others a more than conquering attitude.* **His name (Jesus) has delivered many and entrapped the enemy under their feet.** *There is great power in the name of Jesus. John 10:18 says, No man taketh it from me, but I lay it down of myself. I have power to lay it down, and I have power to take it again. This commandment have I received of my father. Jesus had the power to lay down and pick up His own life. He too has the power to pick you up and to*

The Anointing Powers Of Your Hands

Anoint the works of your hand. No other that has ever walked this earth, has the power like Jesus.

We were not created to be powerless, or to be non-achievers. We were created to be more than conquers because we are created in the image of God. Everything is possible and you will win as long as you have The Anointing working inside you. The enemy cannot control you if you do not allow Him. God wants His force behind you so that the enemy will flee. Everything that you put your hands on, God wants to bless it. **1 John 5:4 says, For what so ever is born of God overcometh the world: and this is the victory that overcometh the world, even our faith.** *God wants you to look on your hands and see Him work at large through you. If He said you could, then it shall be done. Know that JEHOVAH is able. The Anointing is in your hands, so lay your hands on it. It does not matter how big or small, wide or deep God said just lay your hands on it. As you will begin to lay your hands on it, then you will see God work in action. Remember as you move, God will move greater through your effort. If David would have never attempted to fight Goliath, the story could not have*

The Anointing Powers Of Your Hands

been written. It was because of his courage to fight. As he fought Goliath, God gave him the power to win. It is your life, so therefore you must be willing to fight for your freedom. Want to win this battle enough, to fight your way through. Get to work, because your vision wants to live and it needs life. Believe that your hands have the power to do it.

In all that we do we need to be faithful in our doings. I John 5:15 says, And if we know that he hear us, whatsoever we ask, we know that we have the petitions that we desired of Him. Our desirability needs to be strengthen by the putting on of our hands. Saul could not fight this battle because he did not have the faith he needed to win. He had never put his faith in God. However, David had enough faith that saved a whole army. Saul and the Israelites faith were filled with doubt. Though Saul was one of the highest rank military officials, well qualified with many victories He was not capable of winning this battle. The Israelites had it set up in their minds that Goliath had already won the battle. However, David eyes were fixed and immovable on the powers of his living God.

The Anointing Powers Of Your Hands

David had no doubt in his heart; he knew he would win because he was a believer. This is an example that no matter how many attempts to fight the battle, without faith it will be impossible. Without the WORD, how can your faith increase and without increased faith - how is your future going to be victorious? David's faith was so great, because he had the WORD of God positioned right in his heart. So therefore once trouble came his way, he was able to stand on the WORD as it moved his heart to sing a new song. Though he fell tremendously he always found a way to stroke the heart of God. Whether it was through the way David song, danced or praised Him, God was satisfied with Him. When you reach an impossible battle, you will have to have the armies of the living God fighting in you. With just one stone, David killed Goliath. All it took was for him to pick up the stones and to place the one stone in position. In addition, as David placed the stone in his hands God placed His strength in David. Psalms 28:7 says, The Lord is my strength and my shield; my heart trusted in him, and I am helped: therefore my heart rejoiceth: and with my song will I praise him. As David shot the sling, the force was too powerful for Goliath. It in-

stantly killed him. David had the power of God fighting through Him. Notice David only took one shot. His one attempt to defeat the giant was enough to measure his faith. He trusted God so great, until all he needed was a sling shot with one try. David's belief destroyed the giant before he took his first shot. Though the giant was standing in position before David took his first shot, in his eyesight the giant was already dead. David did not use his strength, but His Father's. God used David hands to put His strength in, let God Anoint The works of your hands. Psalms 16:8 says, I have set the Lord always before me: because he is at my right hand, I shall not be moved.

Through the strength of David's hand was the strength of God residing with Him. Just as David, God wants you to look at your hand as a needed tool for survival and conquering power. God armies of power can reside in you. By allowing your hands to work on the vision, you will soon be richly blessed. Faith is movable through your working ability. Many writers have over came their writing journey with the use of their hands. Every warrior that gained the victory has overcome using his or her hands. God wants you to put your hands on it. He will begin to stir up The Anointing and it will be powerful in you. When you put the Lord first in your life, God will give you favor. David desired to please God and He did. You must have a child like heart desire for the Lord. David grew up knowing the Lord as a young boy, and He longed after God's heart. David had a willing heart, not a contrite heart. He did not consider the size of his hands even though man looked at him as just being a child. David never doubted that God could not use Him to fight. Think of a child in the army. He said, yes I will. David achieved through his faith in the Spirit of God. His heart inquired of his next move. He allowed himself to be a witness for God. David exalted God wherever he went and set God needs before his own. He had a unique love for God; David loved to let JEHOVAH know that He was God in his life. Surely you have giants appearing in your life, step up to the plate. Let God use this battle to empower you. Psalms 28:8 says, The Lord is their strength, and he is the saving strength of his anointed. Move and walk by faith and show the world that He has all power. You may look small and be young at heart, but you have a

The Anointing Powers Of Your Hands

strength that is ready to work through you. It is The Anointing and Nothing can defeat The Anointing, because the Anointing destroys every yoke. Get ready to defeat your giants and be prepared to come out on top. As you win this battle, everyone will know that you are a Faith Walker. What if David would have never laid his hands on the sling shot, be a faith walker and lay your hands on it.

The Anointing Powers Of Your Hands

Part Three

The Heart of Your Hands

Beating at Work

"Letting your heart, cause your hands to achieve"

The Anointing Powers Of Your Hands

Sometimes your last resource is always your best. The last shall be first and the first shall be the last. Just when you think things are not going to happen, God will appear. God loves to take the least of all to get the job done right. Hebrews 11:3 says, Through faith we understand that the worlds were framed by the word of God, so that things which are seen were not made of things which do appear. Many people have had the same opportunity as David, but they failed. Saul looked at Goliath and feared. He had all the Israelites standing with him in fear. No one in their human mind would actually stand up to this giant, but David. Out of a whole army, He had the Faith that God would not let him die in this battle. Goliath was a known champion and He had never been defeated. We see things appearing before our eyes and some has caused us to fear the battle, but God wants you to move through your fearful state of mind. God does not want us ever to fear our situations, neither be afraid of going down in the valley. There is power in the valley and you will receive it as you come out of it. David realized it was those times he was in the valley, that he gained greater power from God. Every trial has a wartime and only one will come out a winner. Let that winner be you. If you really want your vision to speak, it is time to fight for it. Now it is your time, to step forward and face your giant. Show everyone around you that you have The Armies of God fighting in you. Often times we have to prove it to ourselves. It is time to pump up your belief, believe deeply in God that your visions are going to speak. Exercise your faith, remember all the many challenges you have overcame with The Powers of God. This faith in God is going to cause you to say yes to His will and yes to His way. David continuously reached for the Heart of God. Regardless of his size, he depended on God to be his help. God gave him the desires of his heart. He has been known to many bible scholars to be listed in The Hall of Faith. Moreover, as many denounced, laughed, criticized and talked about David. God used the smallest one in the crowd and with no skills of basic training to defeat Goliath. Imagine Saul as all the Israelites were standing with Him, none had the courage to go against Goliath. David was not old enough, he did not stand up to their statures

The Anointing Powers Of Your Hands

but David was ready to win this battle. However, in the eyesight of God, David was the perfect candidate to defeat the giant. God knew the size of David's faith. Remind you David was just the Sheppard boy. He was only caught up in the midst because he was delivering food to the unit. Know that God is always in the midst. Though he was small, God fit, all the power He needed in David to kill the giant. God loved the way David loved Him. He adored the way David believed in Him. David knew that God was the one that kept His heart beating through the works of his hands. Psalms 75:1 says, Unto thee, O God, do we give thanks, unto thee do we give thanks: for that thy name is near thy wondrous works declare. God was the center-piece of David's heart.

There must be a time to grow larger than self and the only way you can is to be enlarged through The Anointing Powers of God. David had a re-pentative heart towards God, he was very conscientious about any mistakes that he had made. He never grew too large for God to be his supremacy. He never boasted in self because God obtained the glory. Surely, David made many mistakes through his lifetime. He was human just like you and I but he kept trying to please God. David did not allow his sins or any mistakes to stop him from trying to please his Living GodPsalm 51:10 says Create in me a clean heart, O God; and renew a right spirit within me.

Though we have all made many mistakes we should not let them stop us from trying to please God. Do not let those things stop you from winning your battle. You must begin to work your hands with force. Beating the enemy is God's full purpose for your life. God gains more as you win the victory. Beat the enemy with the good works of your hands. The day that you begin to wash your hands from all vanity is the day that God gains greater glory. You will gain The Power of Righteousness. Everything in your life will begin to come together. God wants Excellency from us. At times, it seems though things can never reach that manner but they can. Your hands are going to possess The Anointing Powers of God. However, they must stay prepared and ready to be used by Him always. Your heart is going to drive your hands to The Anointing. And once your mind is made up in Him then you will do excellent in life. James 4:8 says, Draw nigh to God, and he will draw nigh to you. Cleanse your hands, ye sinners; and purify your hearts, ye double minded.

If you take the opportunity to get closer to God, then surely it will make your visions speak sooner. I remember many years ago in my life, that I went to church through tradition. I never went on my own free will or because I wanted to be there. Perhaps, I went because it was Sunday or I needed a blessing. These are the two major reasons many people go to church. A vast majority only goes when they need a blessing. Going to church was not a priority for me. All those years I went in the wrong state of mind, I could not tell you what the preached message was even before alter call, but I could tell you what the choir song and how good it was. Through those years of my life, I stayed the same and I had no power. Many times, we do not develop in the manner God wants us to because we are not trying to please Him. What is your life speaking today? Do you have a David Spirit or a Saul spirit? God wants you to impress Him. Once you impress Him, then He will cause you to give others a better impression of living life with Him. Many will be inspired and impressed by you. Your spiritual leader is the one that feeds your life. David was fed through His faith and God continuously fed him power to be victorious. Be properly fed through The Spirit of God and stay nourished. David, truly knew God. Romans 10:17 says, So then faith cometh by hearing, and hearing by the word of God.

Some thing's that are causing conflict within your spiritual growth needs to be cut out of your life. I do not believe that many people realize the many blessings that sin keeps them from. It keeps many great things away from your life. If many could see what they miss out on, they would be sick. Love your freedom and love living life itself as God created you to. Understand the word of God and experience real joy. There is so much life in the word, it will keep you empowered. Sin only causes us to suffer more than one way. I have learned that it is not hard to cut sin out of your life, once you begin growing to a greater faith with God. Anything that is crippling your faith or causing you from putting your hands on the powers of God, let it or them go. Get to know who He is. I was held captive for years, all because I did not under-stand His word. However, after I begin to get serious with my spiritual maturity, I grew in the word. It gave my life power. I do not mind offending sin by loving God greater. Sin has held me back long enough. I do not want to offend the God I so greatly love, need and appreciate in my life. Study the word for yourself, so that you can know the kind of God you serve. The Anointing releases you from bond-age, it blesses as it covers your life and it brings forth peace. The Anointing gives you supernatural strength and it will cause you to be a winner always. It destroys the yokes and you will never have to carry another burden for the rest of your life. It will completely take care of you. Is sin really worth The Anointing? Romans 10:17 says, So then faith cometh by hearing, and hearing by the word of God.

The Anointing Powers of God will flow through your hands. Want to stay close to Him, know that cleanliness is next to God. Lay your hands on the things that God would have you to. I want my hands to be clean and pure for God, so that He can operate His anointing in me. One day I received a dying emergency phone call and God told me through my prayer life that I had an anointing in my hands. He said, "for anything to work that I must lay my hands on it." Now going to this hospital for this dying emergency I needed God right then and there. Often times, people need God vessels to stay pure. Moreover, God needs us every second of the day to be prepared to be used of Him. If we are too dirty to be used our prayers may not be answered as we need them to be. This was an emergency and only The Anointing could heal this child. Imagine if I would have been living a double minded life, waddling in sin. Perhaps, The Anointing would not have been able to work through me in prayer for this child. On the other hand, what if I did not know the word of God, I would not have trusted Him myself. It is more power than you realize in the word of God. John 1:1 says, In THE beginning was the WORD, and the WORD was with God, and the WORD was God. The Word gave me a purpose and a reason to stand, just as David. In any emergency, you need The Anointing ASAP. I needed the Armies of The Living God to ride with me, walk with me and to fight for this child's healing immediately. I prayed for this precious child. This child was in intensive care not expecting to make it and the family needed God right then and there. This was a dying emergency that needed The Holy Ghost immediately. I felt the power of God flow through this prayer to heal this child. I am a firm believer in prayer power because it is the Holy Communion between God and His ordained vessels. If I was full with sin, then probably God would have not used me. However, that child needed The Anointing immediately to work powerful in healing her body. It took everyday of the last six years of my life to reach this kind of Anointing with God. I refuse to allow a sinful nature to come to destroy The Anointing that God has bestowed on my life. I refuse to let a little measly three-letter word control any blessings that God wants to bestow in my life. In addition, I refuse to jeopardize my eternal glory to walk on the streets of Gold and destroy my life. Now you can either seek God first at everything in your life or perhaps you can keep letting The Anointing just pass you by. Do not allow a sin to control, guide, lead or the enemy to prepare your future. God deserves that Glory, just give Him your heart daily. Mark 7:5 says, Then

The Anointing Powers Of Your Hands

the Pharisees and scribes asked him, Why walk not thy disciples according to the tradition of the elders, but eat bread with unwashen hands?

One day God enlighten my heart and it begin to long after the word. Then I begin applying every word that I received to my personal life, because if one receives the word then it needs heart application. No one can grow larger in the word without it being a heart application. The word of God must move into your heart and take root. Once it takes root, then you will gain new life. If you do not have self-control, then the Word of God will teach you discipline. It will cause your heart to desire after righteousness. James 1:8 says, A double minded man is unstable in all his ways. There will be a remarkable change within your life. You will change for the better and you will not be the same. Your ears will not want to hear the things they use to. Your legs will not want to walk in the places they used to go. Your eyes will not look on the things in the manner they use too. In addition, you will have a change of heart on many things in your life. Your

The Anointing Powers Of Your Hands

life will have a purpose to love God as you will desire to please Him. I am a firm believer that many people go to church in such a familiar way (traditional). Nevertheless, many have forgotten to seek the way that God wants us to worship Him. I cannot seem to praise God as my mother did because I had to find my own praise. I cannot clap my hands like my aunt, because I had to feel the power of The Anointing clap through my hands. We cannot look on our fore fathers and the way they worshipped God, for we must find Him for ourselves. You must worship Him, as The Spirit of God will teach you how. John 4:23 says, God is a spirit: and they that worship him must worship him in spirit and in truth. No matter how righteous we grow in the word, there is a need for continuous washing of your hands before eating of the bread of life. You want to be pure and ready for God. Go to church with a mind prepared to receive Him as He will feed you wisdom. Get involve with the service and be inspired through the word. Treat the Word of God, as your daily food, it will feed you new life. It will nourish your soul and lift your spirit. The Word will cause you to run when you want to quit. It will fill your heart with inspirations and keep you working on your vision. It will feed you hope in a hopeless situation. In addition, it will strengthen you where you are weak. The Word of God will bond you with The Anointing. That nothing on this earth, will separate you from the love of God. Romans 10:17 says, So then faith cometh by hearing, and hearing by the word of God.

I had to find my way to God by the putting on of my own hands. I had to open the word of God for my self. Lay aside the things that will cause you to reject your personal faith growth. Research things on your own to grow spiritually. Many things I had to leave behind. I could not serve God as my parents did, I had to find my own way with the reaching forth of my praise and with my hands. I am not a firm believer in many traditional things because I never wanted to make tradition a God in my life. I believe in the God that I serve. He is so powerful, loving and caring. He will nurture your soul with righteousness. Know that He takes excellent care of your needs. God wants you to reach high for Him with the putting on of your hands. He will show you the way to The Truth and The Light. Let Him shine through you. Ecclesiastes 9:10

The Anointing Powers Of Your Hands

says, Whatsoever thy hand findeth to do, do it with thy might; for there is no work, nor device, nor knowledge, nor wisdom in the grave, whither thou goest.

The only thing that is keeping your hands from working is you. It is up to you, and it will only be achieved through the measure of your faith. I am going to work my hands since I have the strength of God in them. Want the works of your hands to achieve in the might of God. Nothing should stop you from receiving The Anointing. That life you are dreaming about can either be a gazing dream or you can begin reaching forth with the bareness of your hands, to obtain it. Let your vision be set free. You need your hands to work towards this vision and your fingertips to grasp this moment of hope? God would not have given them to you. Just think of your index finger and everything it is willing to point out to you through the power of God. However, remember as you grab, just place it within the centerfold of your hands and begin to notice God as He will work in you. Hold on to the promise that God has given you, because it is all in the palm of your hands. The more you will begin to use what God has given you, the sooner you will be able to see Him work through you. In addition, as you begin to work this particular thing just watch how God will begin to anoint the works of your hands. God wants you to keep your hands clean, so He can bestow greater power in your life - beyond your imagination. God wants us to use our hands not of our own might but through His might. Work through His might and see that it has already been done. You must believe in the powers of God. Jesus did and He received all power in His hands. He worked His Heavenly Faith. Let your faith work for you, it will take you as high as you believe. Your faith will pull you out of every valley that you enter. It will cause you to win every battle and you will be more than a conqueror. Faith has no limits.

Understand that through your might is inspiring hope and through hope is your power. It will increase your faith possibilities. Every time you think of the works of your hands, do not look at the work of your hands as impossible. Look on the possibilities, if you use them correctly. Your hands have a strength that you need to exercise daily. The vision that God has embedded in your mind, use your hands to work it. Habakkuk 2:3 says, For the vision is yet for an appointed time, but at the end it shall speak, and not lie: though it tarry, wait for it: because it will surely come, it will not tarry. The Anointing will bring you out of all that you are going through, just use your hands.

Often time's people that are striving for something strive too hard of themselves and not enough in God. Striving in self will destroy your vision, but working with The Anointing will bring it to pass. God wants us to strive to believe that it is all possible and He wants us to live life in abundance. For many of years I tried by my own might and I continued to fall. I realized that all the visions God had given me, it was through His will. I struggled to strive. I analyzed every possibility and I kept coming up with remarkable ideas. Nothing seemed to be working out. I had to learn patience. James 1:3 says, Knowing this, that the trying of your faith worketh patience. No, we do not like to wait, especially when we want things to happen right now. However, I learned to be patient with God. As God gives us vision, He will then give us a plan. Only through His power shall the plan be developed. Remember when God give you a vision it is greater than you. So therefore, you will need His assurance for protection of your vision. God does not intend us to overwork ourselves until we are purely exhausted. He intends us to rely on Him. He loves being God so therefore, let Him be the God over your vision. Let Him work His anointing powers through your hands. God is going to astonish you as you see it develop with your eyes. This work is going to simplify many things in your life and bring closure to your giants. John 13:3 says, Jesus knowing that the Father had given all things into his hands, and that he has come from God, and went to God.

All the works, that Jesus accomplished it was The Anointing that worked through Him. Jesus sought the direction, approval, and guidance power from JEHOVAH before He made a move. Heaven was His strength as He earnestly prayed. Regardless of what accomplishment Jesus did, it was all done to glorify His Father. Jesus intended His Father to strengthen Him at everything leaving Him out of nothing. We too must ap-

pear to God in the same manner as Jesus, reverencing Him. He simply followed His heart and He gained all power. God needs to be in full control over everything in your life. Your prayer is your strength and you can accomplish nothing perfectly out of this life without God's full gratitude and permission. If God is in it and if God gave you the vision, then surely God is going to be your help. Jesus earnestly prayed unto His Father. He did not stop until God spoke to Him. Often times we pray, but we do not give God the opportunity to speak back to us. Many say it does not take all day to pray but it may take awhile for God to speak back to you. I do not believe in putting a time limit on my prayer neither do I like to rush my prayer. It is just as rushing someone out the door because you have something else to do. We should not allow anything to hinder our prayer life nor to rush our communion with God. Sometimes God takes His time to listen and then He speaks to us. Kneel down with an expectancy to finish hearing from the Lord before you prepare to get up off your knees. Just imagine, if Jesus would have gotten up too early off His knees as He talked to God. He would not posses all powers today. He would not have given God the *opportunity to instill heavenly power inside Him. Think of how much many has left at the prayer table, all because many did not take the time to listen to God as they have rushed their prayer. Mark 14:38 says, Watch ye and pray, lest ye enter into temptation. The Spirit is truly ready, but the flesh is weak.*

Jesus knew that His life was only because of His Fathers power. So therefore, He never had to analyze or wonder when He needed to pray. Everyone in this world needs The Power of Prayer to make it through. Just as you and I, Jesus had to overcome many things. He suffered tremendously, people went against Him and He too had a mission. It was to save you and I. All because of your vision, many will be encouraged. You need The Power of prayer to get you through. Jesus was very tentative unto His Father through prayer. Jesus needed Heavenly Powers to conquer the world and God gave them to Him. He will also give you the power to conquer. Every work was because His Father led Him first, guided Him through and gave Him the power to achieve. He listened to Heaven as He prayed. Many have asked the question,

The Anointing Powers Of Your Hands

"How do you know when God is speaking to you". Truly it cannot be explained, for everyone hears Him in a different manner. However, you will know His voice. Once you believe that your prayer has reached heaven, then He will speak clearly to you. You will hear Him as you will begin to follow God. As you kneel, be prepared to hear what God has to say to you. John 10:27 says, My sheep hear my voice, and I know them, and they follow me. Your prayer life is of your own free will. The power that God will bestow in your life is up to how much power you are going to need in a lifetime. Jesus made sure He received all the power He would ever need. Jesus suffering was greater than anyone that has ever lived on this earth. God had to allow it just to prove to you and I how powerful He is. No other could have possibly endured what He did, because of who He is. When He raised, so did many peoples faith. His reward was greater than His suffering and His name is the greatest of them all. He continuously knelt down in prayer and God continuously gave Him power.

I needed the strength of God to help me stand against the wiles of the devil. I also needed the strength of

The Anointing Powers Of Your Hands

God to help me continue in ministry. I could not walk as a minister in my own power for I needed heavenly powers to help me. God is the author of my life, He gives me power. I cannot defeat the enemy without the Spirit of God. The enemy will choke you down if you do not have heavenly power. Hebrew 12:2 says, Looking unto Jesus the author and finisher of our faith; who for the joy that was set before him endured the cross, despising the shame, and is set down at the right hand of the throne of God. He wants your hands to be strengthening with prayer power for the work to be completed. God wants you to seek His face and pay great attention to Him for He speaks power into your soul. As you prepare for your new prayer life be prepared to receive greater powers from heavenly places. They will inspire your spiritual growth, well as others that are around you. God is ready to give you heavenly powers that you never knew. Be prepared to do the wondrous works by the putting on of your hands with the anointing powers of God. He is a God of action and as you begin your new prayer life, God is going to act on your prayers. Just remember never to stop praying for it quenches your spiritual growth. Con-

The Anointing Powers Of Your Hands

tinue to pray everyday as though you are praying for the last time. From this day forward, you will become more powerful. Know that God moves as we pray and He listens as we speak to Him. Heaven will hear you, as it will open the doors of blessings to cover your life. Jesus knew the many secrets of God and He received His powers. Get to know the secrets of JEHOVAH as Jesus did and be empowered. John 17:2 says, THESE WORDS spake Jesus, and lifted up his eyes to heaven, and said, Father, the hour is come; glorify thy Son, that thy Son also may be glorified.

Part Four

Spiritual Inflammation

"Let The Anointing, give your vision life. Just, lay your hands on it and your vision shall live."

The Anointing Powers Of Your Hands

*Your prayer life is about to be appealingly altered to a spiritual inner since. God reveals His secrets to the righteous, just be patient with Him. James 1:4 says, But let patience have her perfect work, that ye may be perfect and entire, wanting nothing. What you want is what you desire. What do you want out of your life? A smothered vision will not get you - your heart desires. Let your vision breath, uncover it and allow The Anointing to unleash all it's possibilities. Stop depriving The Anointing to bless your family. Once your faith is unleashed, then you will want for nothing, everything will be entire in your life because the limits will be removed. Prayer will unite a flame within your heart that will cause a reaction for God to move within your life. As you pray, God wants you to feel the flame of His power moving all in you. I consider it to be Spiritual Inflammation. God wants to move as a flame of fire in your **prayer life as The Holy Ghost, will refine you**. Your prayer's are going to reach Heaven in a manner that The Anointing will consume the forces of all your enemies. It will be as a piece of paper, that has fallen* *into a fireplace and it is at its highest blaze. The more you pray is the more God will begin to exalt power in your life. He will give you revelation. Psalms 88:1O says, LORD God of my salvation, I have cried day and night before thee:*

David continually cried out to God because he needed to constantly be strengthened. Though David fought many battles, he needed Gods strength always. It is alright to cry out and to let God know that He is your strength, one could not survive without Him. David wrote many Psalms as he earnestly prayed. Out of the abundance of David's heart, he song God a new love song. David inspired heaven, how are you trying to inspire God? He simply always longed after the mercies of God. He needed to continue to endure his many life challenges and he constantly overcame. When you need to endure, just pray. God will give you what you need. David wanted freedom and every time he called out to Him, God simply freed David. Colossians 4:2 says, Continue in prayer, and watch in the same with thanksgiving.

The Anointing Powers Of Your Hands

Often too many times, we look on ourselves as being all-powerful, because we do not take the time to kneel down. Prayer is an open relationship between you and God, because as you speak He listens and as He speaks then you can hear. In addition, as you pray then you are letting Him know that He is your God. To achieve a greater accomplishment you need The Anointing. A sure way to receive the Anointing is to have a communicable two-way relationship with God. Speak to Him and He will speak back to you. However, you need to watch as you pray so that you can hear Him. Luke 21:36 says, Watch ye therefore, and pray always, that ye may be accounted worthy to escape all these things that shall come to pass and to stand before the son of men. How can you hear Him if you do not take the time to listen in prayer? Be considerate of God as you pray, He wants to speak too. Always expect a response from God in prayer. You must pound on Heaven doors like it is an emergency. Prayer will open the floodgates of Heaven when you are praying in the Spirit of God. If you would take the time to exercise your prayer life, then God will build you with His anointing. Your faith will simply become stronger. The

The Anointing Powers Of Your Hands

Anointing will cause you to have powers from heavenly places. As we grow, we must become wiser. Are you tired of unanswered prayers? Pray until God change everything in your life. I learned not to settle for less, especially when I realized that God has all power to give me the best. God never created us to settle, prove your belief to Him and show Him your faith. Expand your level of belief by trusting God more and expect to live a greater life. James 1:12 says, Blessed is the man that endureth temptation: for when he is tried, he shall receive the crown of life, which the Lord hath promised to them that love Him. Though it may take you a little longer to get what you want, remember He saves the best for last. Ask, what you want and He will answer you. Sometimes I do not ask, because God will just simply give it to me, before I ask. Believe that you are special to Him and He will treat you exceptional. Seek God in prayer until you get His attention and He will inflame His spirit in your life. Ecclesiastes 4:5 says, The fool foldeth his hands together, and eatcth his own flesh.

In the beginning of my prayer life, I never understood why I loved to pray at night. Often times, I found myself kneeling in the midnight hour. Even sometimes, as I was sleep. I would wake up out of a dream and begin kneeling in prayer. Oh, Prayer is the most traumatizing time of your spiritual growth. Prayer will develop a special bond between you and God as you will grow powerfully. It will inhabit your life without notice. I say that because many things will begin to happen. I often thought I was losing my mind when I begin to hear voices speak to me. Then times I was in church, I begin seeing things and I would often know things before they happened. Prayer will introduce you to the Spirit of God. It does not matter how you feel, if your body is tired, aching, or even if you are deep in a sound sleep. Many times, I did not feel like praying, but something powerful moved me to pray. It was unexplainable what came over me. It was a particular prayer, one night that drove me into The Anointing. Perhaps it was because I just needed to catch up with my prayer life.

Often times, many people pray, but not in The Spirit. Sometimes you do not realize how selfish your prayer life can be. People think prayer is only for

The Anointing Powers Of Your Hands

when they want a favor or they have a need. God just wants us to communicate with Him; He wants to talk to you. Just as you desire true and honest relationships in your life, then so does He. In addition, just as you want someone to listen to you, God wants the exact same thing. John 10:27 says, My sheep hear my voice and I know them, and they follow me. As The Spirit of The Lord speaks, His children will know Him. Too many times God is ignored by people, that simply does not want to listen. All because they know it all or does not care to hear Him. Well one thing I know, God is not going to make anyone listen to Him. Anyone that desires to be heard by Him will eventually follow God. Psalms 88:2 says, Let my prayer come before thee: incline thine ear unto my cry; David wanted God to hear him, so he prayed and he prayed. He too had experienced many troubled times, but He could not let his troubles over take him. David trusted God, to listen to him. When you begin to pray more spiritually to God, then spiritual change will intercede with an utterance from on high. Things will begin to change, and you will receive power. God will listen, if you take the time to speak surely He will answer you. God wants you to give your troubles to Him. God will save you in the time of your need, just depend on Him. He does not expect us to do things on our own. However, He does expect us to need Him always. Prayer invites The Spirit of God to be your life protector; He wants to enlarge your steps. Psalms 18:36 says, Thou hast enlarged my steps under me, that my feet did not slip.

David was covered in the Lords grace. Though many ran away from God because they were too busy noticing their faults, David still ran to Him. Many are still running today. David knew there was only one to deliver Him and it was JEHOVAH. He did not mind calling on God, after all God had carried Him through so many troubling times. David figured if God brought me through that, then surely He could get me through this too. God wants us to have the same spiritual mentality as David, never to doubt Him. He wants our trust to be stronger in Him, so that He can increase our territory, enlarge our steps and bless us more. But how can He bless us if we do not trust Him?

The Anointing Powers Of Your Hands

John 5:25 says, Verily, verily, I say unto you, The hour is coming, and now is, when the dead shall hear the voice of the Son of God: and they that hear shall live. God will speak to you, but first He just wants to hear what you have to say. It is just like meeting someone that you really do not know, instead of you doing all the talking just listen. I have noticed, that if you listen to what someone has to say in the first conversation you will get to know them pretty well. In talking to God, He is able to show you just who you are. He will guide you to the full assurance of The Anointing. Now, many different things are going to be rearranged and fully altered in your life. God has a way of moving things around to get us right. JEHOVAH is a God of change and He loves to decorate our lives. His specialty is to make our lives to become beautiful. He is going to make your life peaceful. However, some ultimate changes must take place in your life. These changes will have to occur in order for your life to be fulfilled. Once God begins to work on you, be prepared for a complete life makeover. Psalms 88:3 says, For my soul is full of troubles: and my life draweth nigh unto the grave. David simply needed Gods help, to pull him out of a world of troubles. Many of times, people cannot accomplish their goals due towards a lack of knowledge in The Powers of God. Only a fool will fold his hands on his vision, but the hands of a wise man will make it. God will give you the strength to follow through with your vision. However, if your faith is not in Him, it will not work. Keep your faith in God, not in yourself. Millions have not made it, due to their unbelief. Many have let themselves down; do not be one of them! The hands of a man that will allow critiquing moments without being offended, will cause him or her to become great successors. Know that only God has given you a vision and it wants to live. Stop allowing the pressures of being a failure to interrupt your vision. That vision that you have must go forth. The truth shall speak through the works of your hands. When you really put your mind on the things that God has allowed so many to accomplish, why should it be too hard for you? God knows and many others, have seen it in you. If God did not think that your hands could bear this particular work, then He would not have given it to you. The vision would not have ever surfaced. 11 Corinthians 3:18 says, But we all, with open face beholding as in a glass the glory of the Lord, are changed into the same image from glory to glory, even as by the Spirit of the Lord. Yes, God already knows every-thing He needs to know about you. Nevertheless, do you know exactly who He is? In the beginning of your prayer journey believe me, your life is going to be completely rearranged. Moreover, you really do not know who you are until God introduces you unto yourself. Get ready because God is going to put a new definition to your name and He is going to define you through your prayer life. You will begin to speak with authority and posses greater powers, than Jesus. John 14:12 says, Verily, verily, I say unto you, He that believeth on me, the works that I do shall he do also; and greater works than these shall he do; because I go unto my Father. God is ready spiritually to develop you. Let your vision raise from the dead. You must go deep to know the true depths of the powers of prayer. You will never pray, live or be the same. There is so much power in prayer, but you have to go deep to receive it. In the name of Jesus, I claim you will receive The Anointing. It is time to speak to God like never before and He will speak in your life and make men just say Awe. Matthew 4:17 says, From that time Jesus began to preach, and to

The Anointing Powers Of Your Hands

say, Repent: for the kingdom of God is at hand. Most parents tell their children to pray, but many never teach them how to reverence the Lord in prayer. We all are raised with some form of biblical stories, personal testimonies and family experiences. The key is what has our elders, parents and family members really taught us about the Spirit of God. Now that is deep. Yes, they spoke of God, but did they explain to us that we must get to know Him in a Spiritual manner. After all God is a spirit. Surely, we have seen somebody pray, and yes, we know how to bow our heads, well as fold our hands while we pray. However, did anyone really take the time to teach you to pray in the Spirit of God? Did they tell you to pray until you feel The Holy Ghost move on you. Also, to pray until God say that He is satisfied? That only comes after you feel The Anointing. Did anybody tell you how the power of prayer really works and why you need to pray? Most of us just heard, remember say your prayers before you eat, say your prayers before you go to bed and pray when you wake up. Others wrapped it up and said, "Pray three times a day." I tell many when you kneel down to pray regardless of how long it takes, just pray until you feel The Spirit of God move all over you from the inside out. Prayer is not something that needs to be rushed. It is the most delicate part of your spiritual growth. To be a true life achiever you will need The Anointing. Prayer will ultimately improve your life. John 4:23 says, However, the hour cometh, and now is, when the true worshipers shall worship the Father in spirit and in truth: for the Father seeketh such to worship him.

God have been waiting on you all your life, just to notice that He is God alone. God loves attention, His authority and He wants to be glorified. God wants a personal and true relationship with you that no man can ever depart or interrupt. He wants to answer your prayers, just so you can believe that He is God. He simply wants to talk to you. God loves it when we acknowledge Him. He loves receiving glory. He wants you to inherit a life that will be richly blessed. I often tell people that God just loves to show off His working powers in us. Through your prayer life, God is going to restore many things that you have lost. He is going to work everything out, just as He has always done in your life. Try praying to God, as you

The Anointing Powers Of Your Hands

know Him to be your life restorer. Release your heart to God, it will be the best thing that you have ever done. Psalms 89:17 says, For thou art the glory of their strength: and in thy favour our horn shall be exalted.

Prayer is the holiest communion that any one could ever have with God. He loves the ones that reach towards His heart through the good of desiring Him. Prayer, comes from the heart - it is your heart to heart communication with Him. God loves us to kneel down in prayer to Him, it is just like visiting someone and they are glad to see you. Have you ever been in a relationship and enjoyed that particular person, but really with all honesty you never loved them. If they are there, who cares and if they are not then who cares. But as you grew lonely, you thought about them. It was all for a selfish and personal gain. Shortly afterward, you do not care again. I know it may sound harsh, but the truth is the truth. In prayer, most of us are too busy speaking and we often do not give God the time to say a word. God wants us to feel His presence, and become closer to Him. Many people just bicker, complain and tell God what they need - want or desire.

The Anointing Powers Of Your Hands

Occasionally after finding themselves begging, Lord please help me. What about this one, Lord if you do this for me then I will do that for you? Heaven is not a bargain shop and God is not a beggar deliverer. Stop trying to bargain blessings from heaven. Most people prayer life is like the man on the street corner that holds up the sign, I will work for food. Often I want to tell them, to go to work. Stop wasting your time with begging and bargaining with heaven. In addition, when you talk to Him know that He is listening. God should be worth more than just another blessing. This is a part of spiritual development that we all need improvement. Galatians 3:11 says, But that no man is justified by the law in the sight of God, it is evident: for, The just shall live by faith. Be ready, excited and wanting to feel His Spiritual Touch. Every time you kneel down, you are reverencing His worth. Care about how you make Him feel. Psalms 68:19 says, Blessed be the Lord, who loadeth us with benefits, even the God of our salvation. Selah.

We should never hesitate to bless God in anyway. He is our life creator and protector. I could never imagine being selfish with my mother, after all she has truly been there for me. Why is it so hard for people to bless God? We should never hesitate to bless Him. He is loaded with your every need and no one could supply you as He can. Can you imagine driving your truck up to a dock and someone will begin to fill it with your every need? Well heaven is loaded with all your needs. Think of an empty bank account, better yet one that is over drafted. God has the power to transfer any amount at any time to any account. He is the owner of the largest transporting service in the world, He moves extremely fast. Actually His moves are so swift, you can't see Him as He delivers your blessings. Let your love for Him be beneficial. If you take the time to properly love Him there will be many Anointing Advantages.

Daily God waits on us, preparing that His faithful will come forth. He blesses us, more than we truly deserve. He loves to be glorified and deserves greater respect. God wants full respect and He loves it when we spend quality time with Him. He blesses us every single day of our life that we still have warm blood flowing through our veins. Though we expect Him to always bless us, how often do we truly bless God? Daily He allows us to wake up in our right state of mind, one more day we all can remember. Most people simply take many days of their lives for granted. To live, speak, pray, gain knowledge and to know your own name is a privilege. Every time we open our eyes and see throughout the day, we are blessed. God touches our limbs to be strengthening enough to move everyday and that is worth a moment of true worship. Daily he we are fed for nutritional purposes and daily He shelter's us, that is another reason to truly worship Him. For many of years the enemy did not steal my joy I gave it to him. Every time I did not kneel down in prayer and every time I did not take a moment to worship. God is waiting on you everyday just to worship Him. He does not intend you to wait until you get to church. Show Him honor and bless His name. What if your spouse always love you the same way, take you to the same places and they never increase their love value for you? What if they scorn you, cut out on you or hurt you - do you feel you deserve to be wrongfully treated or disrespected? Well if you only notice Him on Sunday, then He will feel left out.

The Anointing Powers Of Your Hands

Love will always love you back and it will always make you happy. It is time for you to pump up your love volume for Him, after all your actions are speaking to Him. He wants you to worship Him daily. So therefore, when you get to church you will know the truth. You will be able to join in with your praises, as you worship Him in The Spirit. Our prayer life covers us daily. My life I owe to Jesus because He laid down His life for me. So therefore, I am in debt to Him. I take nothing for granted, because I appreciate the God that I serve. No one has done for me or loved me as He has. Jesus laid down His life for you too. If He did not do one more thing, He has already done enough. Honor Him and bless His name for He is worthy. No weapon that is formed against me shall prosper because my Father, which is in Heaven, covers me. Know that He is your covering. God is waiting on you to worship Him in the Spirit and in Truth. A true prayer life opens the truth of spiritual communication between you and God. You will begin to form a spiritual worship just between you and Heaven. The performance of The Anointing is getting ready to show off mightily in your life. He wants to Anoint the work of your hands. God wants to bless every-

thing your hands will ever touch. In addition, He is going to make it all happen just for you. Psalms 88:15 says, I am afflicted and ready to die from my youth up: while I suffer thy terrors I am distracted. We all have been guilty of kneeling just for a need and then as soon as the need is supplied, we find ourselves forgetting to kneel in prayer again. Many times, we have allowed things and people to distract our prayer life. Circumstances to overwhelm our faith and trying times to cause us to doubt. They have caused our spiritual development many distractions. It is time to draw closer to Him and further from the distractions. Many do not really think about prayer, until something happens in their life that will cause them to need God. Often times, many people receive an immediate blessing, but sometimes many do not get what they have prayed for. I have learned throughout the years that if we would not stop praying, then we would not have to keep starting over and over again. When you take the time to get to know God spiritually, the truth will unfold before your eyes. Prayer will build your confidence in Him. That is how simple our prayer life should be with God. Ignoring the presence of the Lord will cause great hindrances in your life. Have you ever called out to someone and they do not answer you? God does not like to be ignored. As God presents Himself to us, He always brings The Anointing with Him. That is the point you want The Anointing to be in your prayer life. James 5:16 says, Confess your faults one to another, and pray one for another, that ye may be healed. "The effectual fervent prayer of a righteous man avail much."

Showing God consideration will greatly enrich your life to become more powerful. It will invite peace to come into your life. Confession opens the blind eyes and your faith will be your sight. When one confesses, it will make the truth appear because their faults will no longer be hid. Often times, many people will not acknowledge their wrongs. However, once one confess with their heart, God will come in and perform miracle after miracle. He will show you things and He will teach you His secrets. God will make all things right in your life. Your vision will gain more power, as your hands will gain Supernatural Strength. The troubles in your life will begin to cease. Your faith will increase in Him and His powers

The Anointing Powers Of Your Hands

will flow smoother in your life. No matter what comes your way, talk to God about it. He listens and as He does, He moves. Prayer will simply cause Spiritual Inflammation to increase in your life. The Anointing will flame righteously through the works of your hands. Regardless of whatever happens in your life, simply do not stop praying. The Prayers of the righteous will always avail, and surely, your vision shall speak boldly.

Part Five

Your Heart Intent

"Following Your Heart"

The Anointing Powers Of Your Hands

God prepares His children to look their best, as He trains them to represent Him with great respect.Children depend on their parents to take care of them. That is how God expects us to depend on Him. God wants us to be prepared for Him, to take care of our needs. Ephesians 6:6 says, Not with eye service, as men pleasers; but as the servants of Christ, doing the will of God from the heart. He is a jealous God and He does not want us to put anything before Him, not even our love ones. God wants us to glorify Him first. He too wants us daily to appreciate Him. For many of years He has tended to the care of our families by ensuring us to wake up in the right state of mind. He has given us the ability to care for them. God wants our attention in Him. Your children see you every day, live with you as you have bent over backwards looking after them. Could you, imagine your child not paying you any attention for days, weeks, months or even years? God wants you to care also about Him, after all you would not have made it this far without God. Matthew 6:6 says, But thou, when thou prayest, enter into thy closet, and when thou hast shut the door, pray to thy Father which is in secret; and thy Father which seeth in secret shall reward thee openly.

Prayer can only surface through your heart, and God knows our hearts? That is why He needs to be positioned first in our life. Matthews 6:33 says, But Seek ye first the Kingdom of God, and his righteousness; and all these things shall be added unto you. When you come to God with a true heart, everything will be set free in your life and there will be no more secrets. Your life will be purposed to satisfy Him. God deserves better from us. He has a better plan for our lives, that is why He gives us vision. He wants us to see that we could have a better life, just kneel down in truth and grow to trust Him. Let God inspire you like never before. For the first time in your life, feel pure and know that your change have begun. Change begins in the heart. It will be like no other prayer in your life, God delivered me and He will do the same for you. When He moves you with The Anointing every UNJUSTLY thing will be served an eviction notice without warning, to get out of your life. Immediately He will put claims over your life and the enemy will flee from your heart. You will never forget that prayer, because that prayer caused your soul to be delivered from hell. From that day on you will have a new start. Psalms 105:15 says, Saying Touch not mine anointed, and do my prophets no harm.

God will touch you and put His Spirit of calmness to live in your heart. If things in your life is troubled, hold on to His word. You have measurable powers in the inside, that are not yet speaking for your life. God is a God of full reward, He even remembers the way we bless Him in secret. Every time we give Him something, He notices the amount of our heart that is wrapped up in our gifts to Him. Give God your best and see Him work greater in your life. He only gives us our heart desires. God gives us the liberty to make our own choices. Nothing can stop or hold God back from working in your life, but you. Satan does not have the power over your future, if God is in control of your life. All you have to do is kneel down in prayer with an expectancy to be delivered. Just kneel with an open heart, and watch God fulfill you. Though some things may

The Anointing Powers Of Your Hands

later try you, God will not let it touch you. His covering will speak to the enemy, touch not my Anointed.

Bow in the need, speak to God with your heart and tell Him you desire to love Him. He will teach you how to love Him, satisfy Him and He will satisfy you. Psalms 90:14 says, O Satisfy us early with thy mercy; that we may rejoice and be glad all our days. Listen to God, He will speak to you and allow Him to lead you into His presence. God loves you and He will satisfy all your heart desires. God said, He will give us our heart desires and when we begin to desire Him every need will be given to us, and every prayer will be answered. Just imagined how powerful that day will be, not just for your life. But for everyone that is exposed to you, that is Anointing Power. God will make you glad. He will change your life in a manner that you will begin to rejoice everyday in Him. 1 Thessalonians 5:17 says, Pray without ceasing.

As you begin to pray, there is no need to stop. Notice every time you stop the enemy forces him self into your life. Put your heart in your prayer. Pray on a daily *basis. Pick a time and place to pray away from distractions. Through the years, I too have begun praying and somewhere along the way I stopped. I had to start all over again from square one. Developing in prayer takes time and it is not going to happen in a blink of an eye. Prayer develops through our prayer experiences. It takes time to build towards a never failing faith. God's timing is different from ours and His paste is at a supernatural flow. Just because you do not see Him move, believe me He is. If God stop being God for a day, tell me how can He supply us mercy in the time of our need. Look around at the hospitals, millions are on life support daily throughout the world. They are living not only by life support, but by prayer support abroad. Through co-workers, church members, friends, family and even sometimes the prayers of a stranger. Many will join their forces together to pray in such a needed time, and God is going to answer some ones prayer. You never know whose prayers God is answering first. I do not know many people that will pleasantly open their front door to a stranger, even after the fact they properly introduce them self. A mother will always know her child, because she would have nurtured*

The Anointing Powers Of Your Hands

her child from birth. You want God to know who you are. He opens His windows of Heaven to look out and see just whom it is calling upon His name. In addition, if it is an unfamiliar voice, then there is much proof you will need to identify yourself. Just as my self, It has taken me years to receive my prayer power. David stayed in touch with God, we too must keep our relationship with Him on very good terms. As you speak to Him on a daily basis, express love to Him and show Him your heart. Just as you need love for your human need, God wants our true love from a spiritual stand point. Reassure Him, that He is the one and only God in your life. The many of tears, prayers, church settings, worship hours, holy communion's and study time in the word, just to reach this point in my life. Surely, God knows us but we must make the effort to know Him. You must continually prepare folding your hands in prayer and never stop the Spirit of God from moving in your life. I cannot count the prayers day and night that I lifted or the tears that rolled down my cheeks. All I know is that God never left me alone, He always answered me. No matter what comes your way, just continue to pray. Pour your heart out to God. Yes, many things are going to try you, keep on praying. The enemy works for a purpose to keep us away from God. Do not give into any more excuses and do not let him separate you from God. Psalms 91:1 says, He That dwelleth in the secret place of the most High shall abide under the shadow of The Almighty.

Jesus gave me the opportunity to a tree of life and I am forever grateful unto God for that opportunity. If you really notice the tree of life, there are branches and connected to every branch there is hope, love, faith, guidance, rewards, heavenly things, divine favor, power from on high, due inheritance, joy, eternal life, blessings assurance, increase, prosperity, salvation, healing, miracles, and everything that is dead is ultimately brought to life. To make it easier for you to understand, daily you and I have the opportunity to receive all these and so much more. An opportunity is not something that is forced on you. It is something that only you can realize the true value of and appreciate it's worth. Accept it with great gratitude within your heart. His presence will then, shadow your ground and cover you always. 1 Thessalonians 5:19 says, Quench not the spirit.

The Anointing Powers Of Your Hands

Every time you have stopped praying, you have allowed the enemy to come to rearrange your life. Know that you need The Anointing. When you stop praying it puts a halt on The Anointing to flow in your life. You have an opportunity to receive the powers of God by folding your hands in prayer. We all have the opportunity to fold our hands in prayer and to gain power from on high. Usually, many give the enemy power over their prayer life by not giving God their heart. Let the presence of God shadow your life. Satan knows when we are not covered. A faithless prayer life intoxicates the blessings that God has for you. When people walk in such stumbling conditions, it is an embarrassment and it's not showing that God lives in you. However, it does show the world that you are off balance, unstable and you are walking without the power of God in your life. The righteous should never live equally to the unrighteous, the world should know who we are in Him. Matthew 12:34 says, O generation of vipers, how can ye, being evil, speak good things? For out of the abundance of the heart the mouth speaketh. It is so valuable for our hearts intention to be correct with God. Whatever is in your heart, will soon come out of you. Your heart must be growing in the right way with God, He knows us by our heart. Many people appear to be good, look well but their actions show otherwise. What are you showing people around you? Would they consider you to be a true God servant and can they identify you as Him being the love of your life? God wants to shadow your life, get covering in prayer. Psalms 91:4 says, He shall cover thee with his feathers, and under his wings shalt thou trust: his truth shall be thy shield and buckler.

Every pence of a second within an hour someone needs God's attention that is how busy He really is. Have you ever realized every emergency that is going on at one time throughout the whole world? God does not have the time to sleep, rest nor slumber. He is a very tentative and watchful God. He is always taking care of His children needs with concern, because He deeply loves them. Do not leave home without prayer. Treat your prayer life, as it is your eternal life insurance policy, make sure you are covered. It is a blessing to keep full spiritual coverage over your life, family, home and future. The Anointing is the greatest life protection you can have, no other can beat it's benefit. It replaces everything that the storms will take, demolish or destroy in your life. Stay covered in the blood. Troubles are always waiting to occur and you do not want to encounter trouble without being fully covered. David was one that was covered with The Wings of God being his shadow. He took the time to love God. That is why he was always covered. When he fell, He was covered as he stumbled. David was covered and as he battled, God covered Him. Make sure you are covered through your day as you leave home and before you lay to rest at night. However, the more often you pray, it just increases your insurance policy with Him. The more you pray it upgrades your trust in Him. Satisfy God with your heart. 1 Thessalonians 5:18 says, In everything give thanks: for this is the will of God in Christ Jesus concerning you.

One thing you must begin to understand is that God loves you. Jesus suffered too much for you to take this opportunity of life for granted. Never take your prayer life

The Anointing Powers Of Your Hands

for granted and never let the enemy scare you. Jesus whole life as He walked the face of this earth was to prove His love first to His Father, secondly to you and thirdly to the enemy. Every work that He did, He uplifted, exalted and glorified Heaven. Jesus is the prime example that you can overcome, you can conquer the enemy with power but you must love Him first. Jesus intended us to pray and love one another as He has. He took the time to teach how to love. All along, He was showing us how to honor our Heavenly Father.

Jesus separated Himself from many to pray and He was teaching us how to follow Him. Jesus took His prayer life serious because He was guiding us to the Kingdom of God and He is the guide to Heaven. You need guidance and The Holy Ghost will lead you as you pray. God has a perfect plan, specifically for you to live. Meaning God wants your lifestyle also to be promoted. He wants others to see how He will bless those that are obedient to His words. Matthews 12:35 says, A good man out of the good treasure of the heart bringeth forth good things: and an evil man out of the evil treasure bringeth

The Anointing Powers Of Your Hands

forth evil things. There are so many people that are watching and waiting on you to make it, they are noticing how God is working miracles out for you. Our life speaks for itself, but is it truly speaking that God lives. God wants you to obtain a supernatural lifestyle that is going to attract many more to kneel down in prayer. You must pray, because your power to overcome is in the way you reverence God. Ephesians 5:20 says, Giving thanks always for all things unto God and the Father in the name of our Lord Jesus Christ. Things may appear not to be going in the manner you would have wanted them, still be thankful. God wants us to appreciate everything in life including the bad. Even in bad things or situations, there is still a lesson. God is in full control of our lives and sometimes He does not always allow things to go the way we want them, because of the plan that He has just for your life. Through the years I've learned to thank God for everything, it's a wonderful thing even during your hard times that you can still thank God from the depths of your heart. 1 Corinthians 15:57 says, But thanks be to God, which giveth us the victory through our Lord Jesus Christ.

The Anointing Powers Of Your Hands

Just imagine if you are giving a certain task, but you never considered your instructions and the importance of them. How are you going to complete your task sufficiently? Surely, you want things good to happen in your life, but are you prepared to do what is needed in order for you to achieve? Be ready to let your heart love in the manner that it will cause others to be set free. John 15:12 says, This is my commandment, That ye love one another, as I have loved you. Grow in a love that nothing will be able to depart you from the love of God. In addition, begin to treat people with greater love, without showing partiality. What you will do for one individual God wants you to do for another. As you will begin to spread more love, then God will be able to reach many more hearts. 1 John 4:8 says, He that loveth not God; for God is love. He enters through our hearts, that is where He lives in us. God is love and we must love everyone always, especially if we are who we say we are in Him. Never can God afford to waste His time. There is a time in your life for everything, and now is the time for a really serious love life with God. Fall in love with Jesus like never before. Begin to care about your love life and the

The Anointing Powers Of Your Hands

seriousness it has over your future, then God will begin to take excellent care of your needs. Once you become deeply concerned with the cares of God, then God gets concerned about blessing your life. So therefore, none of the times can God afford His time to be wasted? God's time is so valuable because when you are not loving Him, believe me that there is someone else receiving His full attention.

God wants you to pray in the truth, not being concerned of big revolving words, but merely just opening your heart to Him. God does not need another person to pray aloud just so others can hear; God needs prayer warriors that are ready and willing to fulfill His desires. Many preachers love to pray openly on the roster, but many of them are not praying in the Spirit. What good is it to pray one day out of the week, just because people are going to hear you. If you have not knelt down to pray all week long, then why pray aloud? Ephesians 5:19 says, Speaking to yourselves in psalms and hymns and spiritual songs, singing and making melody in your heart to the Lord. Allow sweet melodies to flow from your heart to romance the heart of God. Let your heart intentions desire

The Anointing Powers Of Your Hands

to please Him. God knows what is in our secret closet, He knows every time we truly pray unto Him with sincerity from our hearts. Give God your heart and He will anoint the works of your hands. Sing praises to Him and He will give you a new song, as the works of your hands will begin to grow.

Part Six

Praying To The Point of

No Return

"Growing In Prayer Power"

The Anointing Powers Of Your Hands

In order for anything to grow, it takes time. If you want real prayer power, then you will need great patience. First, if you do not sow the seed of prayer, then how can you expect to gain prayer power? Every time you kneel in prayer, you are sowing a seed of trust to God. No one prays to an untrustworthy God. Simply kneel and sow your seed of trust. As you pray from your heart, then you will connect with heavenly power and you will grow in the Spirit of God. Regardless of whatever it is that you want to grow in your life, growing is a process and it simply takes time. Over a certain period, God will enrich your prayer power. I often say that if you want something done right, then you must do it yourself. If you really want God to hear you then give Him a purpose to listen. Begin speaking to God from the depth of your heart, kneel down continuously in prayer. I have learned over the years that sometimes we can exhaust ourselves in prayer. It is due to insufficient trust in God or either we have been disconnected from Heaven. How can you get God to move on your behalf and what is the use of a powerless prayer? It *takes power to surge anything, prayer keeps you connected with heavenly power. Surely, you can flick on the switch, but if the power is disconnected then the lights still will not turn on. If you put the key in your car ignition and turn the key, but you realize the battery is dead how is the car going to start? Without everything being properly connected to its power source, then one powerless thing will stop all power from surging. Perhaps this is the reason some of our prayers are not answered, as we want them to be. Though power from many other sources may be functioning properly, perhaps the way we are currently loving Him, others, respecting each other, worshipping, praising, blessing His name and so on is stopping our heavenly connection to be as powerful as it should. 2nd Corinthians 5:7 says, (For we walk by faith, not by sight:)*

God wants you to be motivated not through your sight but by your faith, encouraged not through your sight but by your faith. And He wants you to be fully prepared at all available times to be able to receive just what He has for you. He wants you to keep your attention on the finished work and not the beginning of the work or even care about the trying times of the work He has given you. He doesn't want you to focus in your own ability, your own strength nor your own capabilities. However, God wants your focus on the heavenly powers He wants to surge through you. The work of your hands are needed to work your vision. Begin planning your dreams to unfold in your life. For many years, I too prayed but I prayed powerless. I thought I was praying as God would have me to, but I realized He was still developing me. Often, we look upon ourselves as being all He wants us to be, but there is still so much room for improvement. A powerless prayer will exhaust your prayer life due towards the fact it's hard praying and still no change. If you really want your life to be changed, then your prayers must change from powerless to being full with The Anointing. In addition, God has all the anointing power you will ever need, just put your hands on it. Get thirsty in your soul for the anointing to overtake you. In order to start anything and especially an anointed prayer life you need power from on high. A certain essence gets the power surging in your prayer life. God yearns for a true prayer warrior, and Jesus was one of the best. I can imagine that He summed *it all up in the model prayer of teaching us how to pray. He had faith that Heaven had already supplied all His needs and ours until this day. His faith caused us to have the same opportunity as His, to live life more abundantly. Jesus never had a selfish heart. After all, He sacrificed His life for us. In the manner He prayed for one, surely He prayed for us all. Therefore, as you pray your heart must be clear to God, because a selfish heart will never reach Gods heart. James 5:16 says, Confess your faults one to another, and pray one for another, and that ye may be healed. The effectual fervent prayer availeth much.*

How is your prayer going to effect heaven as it is answered? Surely many say, in a mighty way but is it what God would want? We pray for many things and often times we wonder why God did not answer our prayer, but He did. God answers us, believe it or not even during the times we think He does not. God hears you. Though we want, desire and yearn for many wonderful things as we pray. God is only going to give us what is best for us. You must be careful what you pray for, because surely He will answer. Though your answer may not be what you wanted, God has answered you. Do parent's give their children everything they ask for, or the things they want their children to have? Just because we ask God for good things, it may not be what He would have for us. He knows best. Think if God would have answered some of your prayers in the past how you wanted them, could you have handled all the consequences that would have came with them? Psalms 81:7 says, Thou calledst in trouble, and I delivered thee, I answered thee in the secret place of thunder: I proved thee at the waters of Meribah. Selah. Just think for a moment. What if you wanted to be a star, though you may have a great potential to be one, you may not be able to handle all the fame. Therefore not all prayers will effect heaven in a good way, no matter how you think it would. Sometimes our answered prayers are not the answer that we wanted, but it is the answer that He wanted to give us. Regardless, in all things, situations, and circumstances we must give God thanks.

You never know when you are going to need a dying emergency from God. It is so valuable to stay prayed up with His Anointing, because it's truly up to how

The Anointing Powers Of Your Hands

much you are willing to value your prayer life with God. There is no since of praying and you have no power. In order to receive power from God you must first crank it up. How can a car start without the key in the ignition and baby you cannot hot-wire a prayer. The key to cranking up your prayer life is to kneel down in the correct way with God. As you begin to kneel, be prepared to kneel down with an open heart. Be ready to confess your wrongs. Surely many people will not confess their faults, until after their addiction has overtaken them. For so long the enemy has entrapped our minds, hearts, bodies and souls because we are not honest enough to confess our own faults. More than often most people are too busy pin pointing other people faults. Wrong is wrong and right is right. It's just like walking into a situation blind folded. However, if so many would have knelt down to pray before they begin their day, then so many would not have experience that demon of addiction, doing something crazy or screwing up their and the list goes on. You never know what will happen in your day that will change your life forever. Many wish they just had another opportunity to go back in time to change what has happened. However, you cannot turn back the clock. That is why it is so valuable to pray before you begin your day. No one, I believe intended to do wrong but many just are caught up in their wrongs and one wrong thing just leads to another. No, God does not want you to dwell in your past, but He does intend for you to do what is right. He wants you to get a new mind set which is to keep your mind on Him. Matthew 26:41 says, Watch and pray, that ye enter not into temptation: the spirit is willing, but the flesh is weak.

That is why it is so valuable for us not to stop praying. We must tune into the Spirit of God first thing. When we open our eyes, whether it is day or night, it's time to pray. Do you ever think to pray for God not to lead you into temptation? Every human being that is truly guilty of their crimes that are sitting in prison or on death row, just imagine if 50% would have prayed the model prayer? Every wrong temptation that is upon the face of this earth is a tempting spirit of the enemy to attack our spiritual development of happiness, good health, wealth and prosperity. God is a God of assurance, love, deliverance, freedom, hope, peace and joy. All of these equal the goods

The Anointing Powers Of Your Hands

that will develop out of your spiritual life through the power of prayer. As you begin to watch you will then begin to notice that, nothing can go forward in your life without the power of God authorizing it and allowing it to happen. See many of us get to a certain point that we cannot bear life as it is and we realize that we want more. But in wanting more you can only get it through God, so now you are prepared to expect a difference in order to receive what you are seeking out of this life. Prayer is so wonderful, because it is so powerful. Prayer is the key to opening God's heart to flow into your life. I begin praying like never before in the year of 1999 and as I prayed this particular night, I did not give it any thought. I just knelt down, but as I begin to kneel down I knew even before I knelt that God was going to hear my supplication. I went to God like never before, feeling of deep urgency and I needed immediate attention. The way my heart felt this night was like no other night I had yet experienced. I longed for God in a manner of confessing my wrongs and all I wanted was for God to make me right. I went down expressing everything from the inside out. I begin pouring out my heart and even until this day, I cannot tell you exactly how long. When I knelt down it was nightfall, but when I rose up the birds were singing and the sun had risen. Within this night of prayer it was the most beautiful night I ever had, I felt poor and needy going down but I rose up with power. I do not remember everything but I know that God was all into it. I know He answered every single need for the rest of my life, just through this one prayer. God felt my heart. I did not kneel down in doubt but I knelt down in true fear for my life, soul and family. I knelt down in faith. I knew what I was but I did not know who God wanted me to be. Only God could change me. This prayer was my life changing prayer; God wants to change your life from being powerless to becoming all - powerful. James 5:15 says, And the prayer of faith shall save the sick, and the Lord shall raise them up; and if he have committed sins, they shall be forgiven him.

You must begin something new that you never have in your prayer life in order to get God's attention immediately. See the Spirit of God is so willing to change your life and as long as there is a will of God surely there is a way. You must not trust yourself (flesh), because you

The Anointing Powers Of Your Hands

are weak and we all need God to help us in our weakest times of life. Even Jesus had to kneel and He is powerful, but He never stopped kneeling to receive His heavenly power. Just ask God to forgive you. Repent from your heart. You must have the same spirit of willingness to pray, so that God can will you His Spirit in the time of your need. Jesus never looked through fleshly eyesight because He was always seeing through His spiritual eyes. Jesus allowed the Spirit of God to feed Him His Spirit daily. Think of it as your vehicle that you drive around the city and your gas begin to run out. However, sooner than later, you will need to fill up again. I think of my prayer life that way because it's a hurting feeling when you run out of power from on high. You never know what situation you might encounter that you will need the power of your prayer to get you or someone else out immediately. Pray earnestly and let God fill you with power. As you continue your new prayer life, the enemy is going to try to grow stronger in your life, because He wants to stop you from praying. However, you just remember that God is larger than all the enemies put together. The enemy loves to throw you off balance and catch you off your guard. Just think, if the enemy can stop you, then your vision will not speak. Think of how many people are going to be delivered out of some form of crisis just because of your vision. One thing you must understand, is that the more spiritually you grow in The Lord is the more powerful you will become. If you have the power of God completely on your side, then the enemy cannot touch you. The Most High All-Powerful God will be guarding your life. The enemy cannot over power God and that is why God needs to be in full control of your life. Luke 11:20 says, When a strong man armed keepth his palace, his goods are in peace.

As you continue to pray, then your prayer power will increase and your covering will shield your area. Many have asked me during the time of our ministry, do you have a covering. Throughout these years, there were so many Bishops and leaders that wanted to cover our ministry but the spirit of God always said to me, "I am your covering." Beginning a ministry is harder than you could ever imagine. Actually accomplishing anything you have never done is going to be challenging, but you can do it. You pray, give and work yourself to the bones trying to

The Anointing Powers Of Your Hands

help people. Trying to get their attention to stay focused on the word of God. In addition, the harder you work, the less they will care to do. All these years with people confessing what God has told them to do for the church and they still do not do it. I sometimes use to get so angry because, I got tired of hearing so many fables and tales. However, as I continued through an almost seemingly impossible fight I realized that I started fighting for a more fervent prayer life. I got so tired of their excuses, and they continued to provide one. One favorite one is that I have to work, for so long I told people the reason you are working two jobs is that you need strength from the Lord. I have never seen the righteous forsaken, forgotten nor left behind. Living life for self will cause forces from the enemy to seclude your mind, praise, prayer life, worship and fellowship. The enemy will try to persuade you that what you are doing is right. I consider it an addiction of confusion, walking blind without power because they know not how to pray. If God has blessed your life and if you keep on your Suit of Armour, you will never have to worry absolutely about the enemy tarring down your house.

The Anointing Powers Of Your Hands

I will never forget this sermon I once heard, "How bad do you want it" man did I grasp it. It's one thing being a Christian, but it is a completely different aspect being a powerful weapon for God. Be a true Christian, prepared to hold down your palace. Be a God listener and a Word doer. There are certain things that I just will not allow to go on in our household, if it were not of God then I could not allow it. The enemy travels through many different ways, but if we stand our ground as we ought to, then the enemy cannot overtake our homes. You would be amazed of how many ungodly spirits many people welcome into their homes. Evil does not care how it gets in. All that matters to it is that it enters. You would also be amazed how many will just openly invite evil. It is easy getting in, but it is extremely hard to get it out. Be careful what and who you invite in your home. Just as well on Sundays everyone must find a place to worship, if I am at church praising God, praying, singing, worshipping, then everyone need to do the same in my household. There is a time in our lives that we must not take any form of power for granted. The enemy has a mighty plan to sneak in our lives, homes and to corrupt our hearts. If he gets in,

The Anointing Powers Of Your Hands

it is a hard thing getting him out without doing a lot of damage. I do not want damaged goods anymore, what about you? If I am praying, then I must train my whole household to pray with me. As for me in my house we are going to serve the Lord. God wants you to stay protected through His spirit and keep daily watch over the things that we allow in our homes. A True Believer must stand their own ground, even when they cannot see clearly they still should stand on the word. You cannot allow any and everything in the world to be in your home. I am a praying woman, over my home and even after someone leaves my home. I believe in the power of prayer, and it is greater to me than knowing my first and last name. Without it, I cannot survive.

I had to realize in my life that absolutely nothing will separate me from the love of God; no excuse is worth coming out of my mouth. No reason is good enough to give to Him and no one is greater to me than He. So therefore, I love expressing my devotion to Him. I believe that when you begin to really care about your prayer life, then you will begin to care about God. Just as many people have asked me, Do you have a covering"? We have had more church people to go against us than worldly people, but I did not let that or them stop me from praying. I looked upon their belief and the way they treated me and I prayed more earnestly not to be one of them, but also for them as well. In addition, God continued to work on my heart.

God blessed us with a building that many thought was a disgrace because of the unfinished, broke down and terrible look the building had. Or perhaps, the way we was representing Him. God spoke and said, "this is how my children make me appear to the world everyday because of their wicked ways". We needed a roof, flooring, walls, electrical work and so much more. We had quiet a few additional fellowship church services. You had better believe more people looked down on us instead of lending us a helping hand. We prayed and sent many letters to churches in Charlotte and to most of those big television ministries, and five churches responded with help. But not one of the television ministries helped, I begin receiving more donation and seed letters from them *than surely I received prayers. We were so grateful how God moved with love through the unidentified, small and the not so flashy churches. However, all the leaders that wanted to cover us never lifted one finger to help, unless we signed our ministry over to them.*

No we did not have to take that church in its condition, but I prayed and asked God for it and He did. I was thankful f or the building that God blessed us with and so was some of the congregation. We must understand how precious our gratitude is towards God because He said that if we can be faithful over few, then He would add all things unto us. In that broken state of a building was Gods fortifying plan for my spiritual growth and development. Our hearts began to grow. Often times, we think our hearts are loving in the capacity God would have them to, but really they are not. Only He has the power to change our hearts as He will teach us how to love. Within these bare walls and a leaking roof God supplied us generous mercy, because we appreciated what He had blessed us with. The power of prayer was able to surge greater power within our lives through the Fountain, that begin replen-

ishing our lives with power. For within this messed up building through many man made eyesight's was the beautiful presence of the Lord. He woke up something inside of me that I thought, I already had. He gave me a heart to yearn for the up righteousness in others that was walking on the outside of this building. There was many prostitutes, drug addicts, children fallen to the waste side and this community was a laughing joke to many. God blessed my heart to feel their need and to want their change, so that many others can see their beauty through the power of God. When everyone else gave up on me, Jesus was there. This job needed the anointing of God to overflow and spread abroad. So then I had to begin a deeper prayer journey. No matter how good you begin to pray you will always need to take a deeper plunge in the Spirit of God. The passion that God has given me to help others is great and mighty. Many of times, I wondered Lord why am I suffering so and when is this vision going to prosper? God would always give me words of comfort. I felt my life was unfair as no one seemed to care, but God was still multiplying the vision in me. The greater your suffering, the more challenging life will become. However,

The Anointing Powers Of Your Hands

once you overcome is the greater your victory will be. You will never forget what God has done for you and you will always be recognized in heaven that you are His. John 17:9 says, I pray for them: I pray not for the world, but for them which thou hast given me; for they are thine.

Truly while many walked out of this ministry because of our heavy workload and the needed amount of finances to operate this ministry - it was heart breaking. The unity that had to be enforced, they missed something that money just cannot buy. Hoping in a hopeless situation as you will endure to the end. As we endeavored living life in many messed up situations, God blessed those richly that held on. Surely it was only a hand full but it was the ones, that was true to Him. Many missed their faith increase. God stretches our faith as we stretch our hope in Him. Instead of putting your eyes on the amount of creativity of your mission, the hardship that it is going to take to make this all possible, just remember that God moves in every impossible situation. While you are wondering why, He is moving. While you are pacing the floor, wanting to believe as your faith will sometimes question you - He is moving. Though many things will try it's best to stop, tare and destroy your vision - God is moving. In addition, when the ones you need to stick by you as you so dearly always depended on them and they walk out - God is still moving. No matter what your circumstance is believe greater in God, never look at your need because God is going to do it. Take your heart off your troubles and be prepared to overcome all your enemies. This victory is yours and know that this battle is already won.

I realized here in this mess of a building that God needed to gain something of me that before I just did not have. Many of our members missed their faith inheritance and spiritual development. God never wanted us to feel the pressure of getting this building done, He wanted us to see how so many souls have been undone spiritually. For this opportunity was one of the deeper faith unities that God has ever embarked on my personal life. Sometimes God will try your heart, just to see where you stand. When Job suffered through great travail, he did not give up. He endured as he suffered and he held out as he waited. But through Job waiting period, he was faithful

The Anointing Powers Of Your Hands

being righteous. In most cases, during our waiting period how righteous are we? Many will sometimes allow their eagerness to lead them into temptation, as they will take their eyes off God. Often times, many people move too quickly and try to rush God to move. If people would learn how to wait patiently on God, then God can properly cultivate their faith and reshape their destiny. Even though God already know you, He just wants to show you something that is going to add greatness through His Spirit to strengthen you with pure powerful faith. As you look on the things within your life that seems impossible I am here to tell you, that it is all possible. I do not care how bad it is just remember, "How bad you want it." If God gave it to you then it is already yours, stop letting the things of this world get you down but allow the powers of God to lift you up. Put your hands on whatever it is that God said for you to do and never focus on the impossibilities of your vision, but keep your mind focus on how God can make it all possible just for you. Luke 14:18 says, And they all with one consent began to make excuse. The first said unto him, I have bought a piece of ground, and I must needs go and see it: I pray thee have excused me Luke 14:19 says, And another said, I have married a wife, and therefore I cannot come. Excuses, excuses, excuses - too many excuses is what many people tend to give God. Their creator and maker should be worth more than an excuse. It should not matter the circumstance or occasion we should never give God an excuse. Every time we give an excuse, we excuse ourselves of new life opportunity. I grew through all their excuses the members that quit, the churches that did not help, the love ones you thought you could depend on and the people that did not support. Because every obstacle that came my way, God just picked it up and moved it. I thank God for everything He has done in my life. However, I knew it all was done through the power of prayer, because God answered me every time. He is my covering because He is the God in my life? For with the power of Jesus as your armor you will gain power far beyond your imagination through your prayer life, as the enemy will begin to tremble as you speak. As I continued growing spiritual in this process, I knew that it was all God and not me. I knew that God listened and answered my prayers. Nevertheless, I could not stop praying, I felt the yoke of Jesus around my neck. I wanted to quit sometimes, but the

The Anointing Powers Of Your Hands

power of God would push me down on my knees and bring me back to remembrance of what He has already done within my life. I know without a shadow of a doubt that Jesus is my covering and that no other man on this earth could cover me like He can. God is the only keeper of my life. The only time most people will help you is when they can get something out of it and I refuse to give them that glory for my God deserves all the Glory thereof. He has been by my side when I could not depend on no one, not even myself. He laid His life down for me, no other has done that. What are you prepared to lay down for heavens sake? When I cried, He wiped my tears away. When I needed Jesus, He did not hesitate - He was there. Many times I felt like giving up, He encouraged me to run on. Through it all. When I looked up and could not see no one else, I was able to see Him working on my behalf. He has been my midnight comforter, my early morning praise, my bread when I am hungry and my noon day life director. He instructs my faith on how to trust Him more. He has loved me greater than any one on the face of this earth and I love Him.

The Anointing Powers Of Your Hands

Often times I just break out in praise because I know Him and when you truly know Him nothing or no one can turn you around. I thank God for His Son all the time because Jesus has truly been my role model. When you realize the power that your prayer holds, peace will begin to surround everything within your life. Regardless of how bad things will sometimes get, you must not focus on the bad but allow God to Anoint your situations. Focus on your defeat through the power of God. It is only available to you in the Spirit of God, through Jesus Christ. God does not want to hear our excuses or bickering complaints, He just wants you to believe that He is. Know within your heart that He is God. Never put anything or anyone before Him. Just pray to the point of no return and watch God work through you. The more you develop in your prayer power is the sooner all your promises will be fulfilled. Remember, the power is available to you, just lay your hands on it and watch Him work through them.

Part Seven

Seven Keys To

Embracing The Anointing

" Clinch On to Him and never let go".

The Anointing Powers Of Your Hands

Imagine if you had all the right set of keys to open every door you needed in your life. I mean never having to wish, want or crave for anything, but having pure power to gain it all. Reverencing your Heavenly Father, because you know He has worked powerfully in your life. Thinking of the many death traps that was set before you. The enemy purposed you to be destroyed. He knows how powerful your vision is and he wants to exterminate it. His mission is to stop you. Your faith is what he wants smashed and your dreams he wants to steal. Every time you have tried to climb higher, the enemy put a snare in your way, as he has purposed your faith to die. However, your faith multiplied because you continued to hold on to The Great I Am. He has comfort you when many trampled on you. The enemy see you as a threat and he does

The Anointing Powers Of Your Hands

not want your faith to survive. He simply wants to take you out. It is time to grip The Anointing, until you squeeze your next miracle out of heaven.

Key One: Respecting Jehovah

Matthew 6:9 says, After this manner therefore pray ye: Our Father which art in heaven, Hallowed be thy name.

Jesus knew that God would always take care of His needs, personally, well as spiritually because God was within Him. Jesus worshipped His Father from His inner soul and adored Heaven from the depths of His heart. His worship was a fervent and private worship that kept Him connected to His Heavenly Powers. It was between Him and His Heavenly Father, He allowed no one else to enter. Your prayer life needs to be private, stop letting every one in. Opening your prayer by honoring Him as worship brings God Spirit into you. His Spirit will move deep in you. The Anointing will begin to caress your soul as you worship Him. Truth will arrive in your mind and freedom will be your morning praise. He will show you the way. Motions of movement will begin to change you from the inside out. Heaven will open, as it will fill you with His presence. The many troubles that hell sent my way. A thought right now of how I made it over, is worth a shout of praise. Though your enemies tried with every-thing to put fear in your heart, you overcame. 11 Samuel 22:5 says, When the waves of death compassed me, the floods of ungodly men made me afraid. God heard you as you cried out in terror, wanting your troubles to cease. God knows it all. We hurt, we have feared and sometimes we have allowed the enemy to stop us. But thank God it was not forever, get back to work on your vision. Nothing or no one should ever attempt to kill the Anointing, be-cause it is The Yoke Destroyer, The Hell Dis-Connector and I also consider it, my Supernatural Hell Demolisher.

Now realizing how hollow your Heavenly Father's name is, it is worth your true worship from the depths of your heart. Calling on Him with respect will cause heaven to speak for you. You will gain power to overcome, call on Him. Jesus wants us to honor His Father, by calling on Him. God will begin to conduct your

The Anointing Powers Of Your Hands

life and He will declare things to flee from you. Notice the scripture, it posses the first key to providing you with the method of receiving Anointing Powers. Just reverence Him. Jesus knew the manner to pray which is the method for our Heavenly Father to be our life conductor. Surely, you know a conductor's duty is simply to take you to your destination. The Conductor is in full control. So therefore, take notice towards this manner, because without True Worship we just simply cannot enter into the presence of the Lord.

John 4:22 says, Ye worship ye know not what: we know what we worship: for salvation is of the JewsFor many of years, many have gotten it wrong as they pray. Though they believe that they are seeking God, truly they are seeking for material possessions. Many are worshipping God in the wrong manner, which simplifies the wrong method of glory. God knows our needs and He has provided greatly for many of us, but often times we worship our blessings, possessions, things and consider them to be miracles as they receive the glory. Allow God to receive all the glory not man made things. Every time you exalt your things, we are giving the things in our life glory and it shortens God of His honor. You must be extremely careful how you honor Him because we want to satisfy Him. God wants you to worship Him, because He is The Great I Am. His name is Jehovah, which is The Most High. He is Jehovah Nissi, your banner of hope, life forevermore. God wants you to worship Him, because He has freed you from bondage and took the keys of Hell through His only begotten son.

Once you know Him in this manner, no one have to remind you to worship. Your heart will be driven with a love passion to worship Him openly, freely, true fully and spiritually. The Anointing will be unraveled within your heart and your life will be explosively blessed. Worship covers your life with His blessings. God is 100% Pure Spirit, His presence will cause you to walk in agreement with Him. God wants you to recognize who He is, respect, honor and exalt Him to the fullest. Worship ushers you into The Presence of Righteousness as God will begin to justify your life. True worship releases The Anointing to destroy the yokes and to tare down all strong-

The Anointing Powers Of Your Hands

holds. It unleashes Heavenly Power to surround your atmosphere and to walk before you. Now as you enter into His presence through your worship, you will also enter into His Kingdom powers. Every time you worship Him in The Spirit, God justifies your life. Just as the woman with the issue of blood, her way of worship was in her press. She had her eyes fixed on her determination to touch the presence of Jesus. She no longer felt her pain or claimed her issues, it was His virtue that drew her near, until she touched The Anointing. Once you begin to worship, you cannot feel anything, but God moving in your life. Nothing at this point will stop you from moving into His presence. Your mind is not your own, your being is filled with freedom and your atmosphere is now in His presence. However, troubles that caused issues to ruin your life will ultimately disappear, no tears of sorrow but only joy as praise will utter out of your mouth. You are now at the point of no return, all things are past away and now the newest has been effectively promised to you. God has ushered you into His presence, where no weapon formed against you will be able to prosper. Your release time is here. The many things that periodically caused issues to come in your life, will not trouble your bridges any longer and no storm will wipe you away. You are now at the point of no return. This is the most valuable key that will cause your prayers to be ultimately heard by Him. You will have supernatural prayer power.

Key Two: Matthew 6:10

Thy Kingdom come. Thy will be done in earth, as it is in heaven.

Everyone dreads the day of Judgment, for The Kingdom of God is at hand. Without God there will be no heaven. Embrace The Anointing. God will reign all these things in your life, complete healing, full deliverance, sufficient grace, perfect mercy, jolly happiness, beautiful joy, abundant blessings, pure faith, greater love, magnificent meekness, caring gentleness, perfect peace, inspiring hope and so much more in your life. The things that God reigns are not man made, but spiritually granted unto His true and faithful. Daily God's will is performed in Heaven as it is on earth. When you are living in God's will, there is no worry. When you pray, say Father let your

The Anointing Powers Of Your Hands

will be done in my life, because through every will there is a sure inheritance. Daily I want God to will me my true inheritance, what about you? The only way to be included in a will is that someone must favor you. They must want something greater for you to have, because they have seen that you deserve it. In addition, you are very special to Him. I do not know anyone that will just will anything to anybody without knowing them personally. Allow God to notice your work effort.

As you seek God in prayer, you will notice that everything He has allowed in your life was perfectly fit for you. Surely, everything that He will begin to do in your life is perfectly designed just for you. Allow God's will to be done in your life, for He knows what is truly best for you God knows your needs. He knows your wants and He will give you - your heart desires. God is a perfect and He is the Father of perfection. Allow His will to be done in your life is the second key to possessing anointing powers. He will bring you heavenly things that the enemy will have no control over.

The Anointing Powers Of Your Hands

Key Three: Matthew 6:11

Give us this day our daily bread.

You want God to properly feed you, as The Anointing will nourish your life. Daily you need a word to support the true factor of God and not only needing that daily feeding just for nutritional purposes, but more for spiritual development. Study His word. Within the word of God, there is life more abundantly. Power is in the WORD, that will incorporate your life to be abundantly satisfied. Matthew 4:4 says, But he answered and said, It is written, man shall not live by bread alone, but by every word that proceedeth out of the mouth of God. You want God to give you exactly what He knows that you need. Many of times we go and supply our own needs and never realize until it is too late, that God did not intend us to have it. God is a perfect provider. He is not going to give you too much if you cannot handle it yet or if you are not prepared for it. He will properly proportion your life to the way you deserve to live, after proving to Him how well you handle life itself. Understand some people receive blessings that sort of give them the big head, their atti-

The Anointing Powers Of Your Hands

tudes change and they forget all about God. In most cases, some people just cannot handle success, blessings or gain. So therefore, as God will begin to bless you remember how you received it, who gave it to you and never forget where He has brought you from. Just because you receive your blessings continue to bless God, never put Him on a back burner. Daily I want God to provide me with what He wants to provide me with. Man cannot live by bread and water alone, but by every word that proceeded out of the mouth of God. Daily let God feed you. Hunger for more of Him. Truly, His word is real and it will set you free. As you pray, you will want freedom because in freedom you are able to put your hands on things that will add greater things in your life. There is a certain spiritual feeding that you are going to need, just to get to your next level. It takes time to grow spiritually, but it is up to you to want it earnestly. Spiritually invest into the word and watch Jehovah - Jireh give you power. He is your power provider. The only way to receive The Spirit is to go to God in The Spirit. Go after Go, seek Him daily and pray to Him earnestly. Allow Him the opportunity to grow in your life through the word. Let Him be magnified in you and through you as you endeavor deeper into The WORD of God. Only His WORD can feed you life as it will teach you how to gain access to heavenly powers.

Key Four: Matthew 6:12
And forgive us our debts, as we forgive our debtors.

Regardless of our effort in trying to be true to God, we all tend to make many mistakes. When you seek God's forgiveness, you need to have the same compassion in your heart to forgive others. I have seen family members that consider themselves to be Christians, and friends that cannot forgive each other. Still we expect God to forgive us, then we harden our hearts to people that need our forgiveness and love. I have done so many wrong things in my lifetime that I asked God for forgiveness and He Did. Forgiveness is the most important factors of seeking after the presence of God, It is the fourth key to gaining the anointing. It will cleanse the heart of impurities that the enemy has power over. Mark 11:26 says, But if ye do not forgive, neither will your Father which is in heaven forgive your trespasses. I do not personally want

The Anointing Powers Of Your Hands

to be one trying to appear to God in seeking forgiveness and cannot forgive my own brother or sister. God has no respect of a person neither should we, He equally loves us. Though Jesus laid down His life for us, God expects the same out of His children daily. Moreover, just as we ask for forgiveness of God, then we need to learn how to forgive others. Remember, ever hold a grudge.

Key Five, Six & Seven: Matthew 6:13
And lead us not into temptation, but deliver us from evil: For thine is the Kingdom, and the power, and the glory, for ever. Amen.

God knew us before we entered our mothers womb. God knows our inner secrets and everyone's temptation. Daily the flesh will be tempted, that is why you need self control. You never know what is ahead of your day until it is over, regardless of what's on your agenda. The enemy knows what makes us weak, that is how he tempts us. The enemy is the author of temptation and the owner of deceit, destruction and the largest murderer of all times. Daily Jesus prayed, because He acknowledged that

132

temptation was all around Him. So therefore, Jesus did not want to be lead into temptation and we must pray in that manner. Overcoming temptation is the method of receiving power to overcome all that is against you. If Jesus walked on the face of this earth with great power as He prayed, we too must do the same. God is the only one that can cause you to live in your Divine Purposed life. So therefore, never leave home without praying. The fifth key to obtaining the anointing is overcoming temptation and saying no to sin.

Many people could have had a better life if they would have taken the time to embrace The Anointing. It would have walked before them, covered their day and removed their stumbling blocks. Just as prisoners, drug addicts, prostitutes, liars, cheaters, robbers, murders, molesters, adulterers, falling pastors and the list goes on. It is so valuable to learn the power of just saying no to sin as we stand firm on the word. It will release the fullness of God to be evident in your life. Respecting God only enhances the Kingdom of God to cause the worldly people to desire after righteousness. A true servant of God

The Anointing Powers Of Your Hands

will soon be blessed beyond measures. The Anointing will come on you. Prayer is the one key to everything you will ever need and it is the greatest weapon of defense to make the enemy flee. Expect doors in your life to open that no man will ever have the power to shut.

As you endeavor in prayer, the enemy is going to try to tempt you in every way. He wants to stop you from entering The Kingdom of God. The six key is trying all that you can to enter into The Kingdom of God, for it is at hand. When you really try, then you will truly succeed. The enemy does not want you in the presence of God, because there will simply be no room for him in your life. This is the reason you have to take your prayer to the next level. Let it become spiritual. For many years I thought the enemy was so powerful. However, I realized that God is more powerful than the enemy. When you were a child and a bully always aggravated you, upset and hurt you - eventually you stood up to them. One day you got tired of the bully and told your parents. They rushed to your need and took care of that bully for you. That is how God takes care of His children. God sits high and looks low and He will demolish my enemies. 11 Samuel 22:36 says, I have pursued mine enemies, and destroyed them, and turned not again until I had consumed them. As David went to battle, he was constantly prepared to fight. Are you ready for this battle, if so know that it is not yours it is the Lords. The only way you can win is to attempt to fight. Just as God brought David through each battle, he gained more victory as David's faith was also strengthened. God will do the same for you, continue growing in the power of prayer. Fold your hands, kneel down and watch how God will change your life. Our God is a patient God and His timing is not like ours.

Prayer is serious, devote your heart to God in prayer. I do not know all that He is going to require out of you, just be tentative as He begins to speak to you. I love praying because I love to hear God speak to me. He always encourage my heart, give inspiration and will strengthen you to continue uprightly with your vision. Things have occurred in your life, sometimes tried to alter the way you serve God, but keep on praying. Be thankful that He is your Comforter. Do not run from God any more,

The Anointing Powers Of Your Hands

fix your mind from this day forward to run to Him. So now, through many life experiences I hope you have learned to seek God's approval first and let Him be your guide. He has done a miraculous job in your life, because things could be worst but instead of your many wrongs, God has still blessed you. That work that you must achieve, He said, "Yes you can." Now all you have to do is, put your hands on it. Just because there has been a halt to your work, does not mean that it cannot move forward. God wants your work in progress, so that He can receive the glory of it. As you embrace The Anointing, God is bestowing your future with many new blessings. The seventh key is making sure God receives greater glory out of your life. As time goes on, many should see your great accomplishments, wonderful change and many should be richly inspired to reach more for Him. You should be attracting more and more to desire after The Kingdom of God. I cannot promise you that it is going to be easy, but it all will be more than worth it. You may have to shed some tears, hurt with pain as your heart will ache, but you will succeed if you continue to believe.Embrace   The Anoint-

The Anointing Powers Of Your Hands

ing, it will embrace you back as your new blessings will add luxury to your life.

Part Eight

Getting To Know Your Hands Personality

"They look stronger than they appear"

The Anointing Powers Of Your Hands

I know often times God has given you some form of creativity and as you look over your life, you may see what life changing affect it could have on you. Psalms 50:15 says, And call upon me in the day of trouble: I will deliver thee, and thou shalt glorify me. God expects us to get ahead, instead of barely making it. If JEHOVAH is God over this whole world and owns everything, then I realized I am a shareowner too, just as Abraham. Therefore, I knew I needed to make a change in the manner that I truly praised God. I had to believe more in the talents God had given me, but it could not have been possible until I begin putting my hands back to work, after praising God for these beautiful gifts. God gives us gifts and if we use our gifts to glorify Him, then He will begin to glorify us. God intend for us to use what we have, instead of estimating on things that are not yet in our possession. I realized that I was a nobody to many, then I figured who would want my writings? For many of years I continued to work in my field as a hairstylist. I allowed my family to be hindered of divine prosperity; vacations and even a better *lifestyle of living, due to my insecurities of the writing ability that God had given me. However, one day I realized just as Paul and Silas they never quit believing no matter what came their way. Even when they were thrown into prison, they did not let their situation stop them from praying and praising. Often times, we allow our situations to hold our praise in contempt. When you really want something greater from God, then you need to praise Him to the point of no return. Let your praise cause your next miracle to be released. The more outrageously you bless Him is the more outstanding your reward will be. Alternatively, I begin to believe in a lifestyle that quiet naturally my income could not supply, so then I begin writing more and more. More than enough times in our life, we could have the things that we want if we use what we have. I once heard this pastor speak about pastors writing inspirational books. As He criticized them, it was no different than what He was doing - preaching for a reward. Truly the word clarifies, you will only reap out of life what ever you sow. A authors duty is to write, as a pastors duty is to preach and teach. After all a book will live longer than any author and it never dies. A preached message mostly does* not even leave the church, for the word hardly enters the heart of the congregation. Look around the world, it is speaking for itself. Whose to say who God is using to touch and inspire lives. Actually one day as I was entering the store, this one Pastor said, "Living Life In A Messed Up Situation Volume One is phenomenal, I believe I was more inspired than He was. As I write, The Holy Spirit is speaking through me on paper, vice versa as a pastor preaches, the spirit of God is feeding them. It all works together for the building of His kingdom. Ministry comes in so many different forms, the key is that hearts are motivated to stay rightfully inspired in the Word. I was born to write, actually one of the greatest days of my life was my first book signing. Nothing will ever be able to take that moment from me. For once in my life I finally reached the mark that God wanted me to be in life. So many wanted to know when my next book was coming out. Many were enriched as they was greatly inspired. I am just grateful that I followed my heart and allowed God to use me in any way possible to encourage someone else. I constantly praise Him for every bruised situation in my *life and all my troubled times. I lived life in many messed up situation, but surely Jesus carried me through.*

The more you will begin to work towards your finish, is the sooner you will be able to have what you want in life. God wants us to be great achievers through the word and more than anything God loves to be glorified. No matter the circumstance that you think you are in, know that is how God wanted it. It does not matter how many look down on you, God adores you. 11 Samuel 22:21 says, The LORD rewards according to my righteous; according to the cleanliness of my hands hath he recompensed me. It does not matter how impossible things seem to be, God still wants you to use what you have. God wants to bless your life to the extreme. Stay focused until it is finished. If you are living in a low degree and desire a better life, then you are just perfect for God to use. However, the key is are you ready? If you look like you are not serving God like many others and you do not have great possessions, then you are the perfect vessel for God to exalt. To many as a preacher and writer I simply looked like a joke, but God will have the last laugh. I love giving

The Anointing Powers Of Your Hands

God the praise, because He will spiritually incorporate your life from nothing until it overflows with everything. 11 Samuel 22:20 says, He brought me forth also into a large place: he delivered me, because he delighted in me.

I stopped looking at what I did not have and started praising God for all that He has given me. I knew deep in my heart that God gave me this writing ability and all those beautiful songs and spiritual books was going to set many people free. As long as God can receive the glory, then He is going to make a way for you. Surely, God has given you something and at one time or another you began performing the work, with the putting on of your hands. God does not expect for us to prepare ourselves with things that can quickly fade away. However, God wants us to keep it all spiritual that will cause us to yearn for more. He will continually fill us, as we run out of the things we need. He supplies our needs. Heaven is our warehouse of blessings and it is overstocked. The blessings are ready to be delivered to you, but God is just waiting on your work to be complete. Just as the story of the ten virgins, five were prepared and five was not. The five that was prepared continued to be in a spiritual developing process. They did all that they needed to do, because they followed their instructions being fully prepared and ready. The five that missed their opportunity, stopped caring about their needs due towards their slothfulness.

God will begin to bring forth the things, as we need them for the ones that are prepared and ready. What is the use of having great vision and no true hope? It will not live. However, with hope it is all possible. I allowed book writings, studies, and beautiful spiritual songs to set in the file cabinets for many of years. You think that if you would have finished what you have started, you might not be in the predicament that you are in right now. If God intended it to have already happened then surely, it would have.

David, proved himself mightily to the Lord, since he was a child. Yes, he made many mistakes, sinned over and over again, but David never stopped crying out to the Lord. He was not perfect, he had a lot of problems, but he continued to cry out to the Lord. Life is stressful and it can be very difficult at times. There was many things David needed help and when he did - he called on the Lord. Every time David drew closer to another battle, he begin to call on the Lord. And every time he cried out, the Lord came to his rescue. Psalms 4:1 says, HEAR ME when I call, O God of my righteousness; thou hast enlarged me when I was in distress, have mercy upon me, and hear my prayer. On the other hand, perhaps if you had kept your hands on the vision that God had given you, then you would already be there. Enough with the excuses! God has given you a great gift, perhaps many different gifts. But only, one of them is designed to bring your life glory. We can come up with a thousand excuses, but not one of them is going to truly matter. What matters now is that you stop looking at it all to be impossible for you. Let Him make many wonderful things happen in your life. 11 Samuel 22:4 says, I will call on the LORD, who is worthy to be praised: so shall I be saved from mine enemies. God loves impossibilities and He loves us to look upon Him for our help. Whenever you are in trouble, all you have to do is call upon Him and He will be there. He is only a prayer away.

The Anointing Powers Of Your Hands

Stop wasting precious time analyzing your personal situation. I had to experience spiritual growth in order to mature in greater works for Him. I no longer wanted to be just a writer, but I longed for the desire to encourage many hearts to run towards their vision like never before. Romans 12:12 says, Rejoicing in hope; patience in tribulation; continuing instant in prayer. Just remember if God gave it to you, then you can accomplish it. I do not believe that God give wasted or lifeless gifts, appreciate what God has given you. Use what you have and learn to work it.

There will be times that will occur that something might traumatize your prayer life. When you are traumatized, some things happen without notice. Expect a breakthrough to bring you out. You may either go deeper into prayer or you can get in a state of shock. In some cases, people have found Jesus in a wounded situation, because it caused them to do something for God that just was not expected of them in a normal situation. In addition, in some life shocking changes some of us know that we cannot do it, but God can and will. I think that is how Paul & Silas felt when they were thrown into prison

The Anointing Powers Of Your Hands

just because they were believers in Christ and carried the word of the Lord in their hearts. In this unexpected imprisonment, they had no time to complain, bicker or feel their weakness. They knew without preparing to think that this was a time for rejoicing and praying. In many of our life experiences, we analyze why, how and when. I tell many forget that, because it has already happened. Now is the time to pray and to move forward. Your situation that has happened needs to be over. You can never erase your past, because it has already occurred. However, you can start the effectual change with your present right now. Now is the time to pray, so that God can change your future. God loves to show up in a hopeless situation and He is our hope living life in a messed up situation. This hope is God's specialty.

I know you may be thinking yeah right, how are your hands going to show forth a personality? How can my hands speak for me? Well in every way of your life, if you notice a homeless person you never think of how they got in their position. The first thing you notice that their live's seem to be seriously in the need. Generally

The Anointing Powers Of Your Hands

classifying most of the homeless, neighborhood drunks and so on, they appear to many people just to be bombed out. How many times have you past by one particular person that was living in a low degree and you were greatly inspired by their life achievements? Did you desire to be like them? I am not talking against them, because the majority of them realistically was not prepared for their falling situations. No one desires to wake up and ruin their future. Perhaps, they were alone and did not have correct association to keep them inspired during their hard times. The main thing I want you to understand is that you never know what is going to happen in your tomorrow, that is why it is so valuable to fully prepare your future with the word today. Let it speak through the works of your hands. We drive by and pass plenty that are beggars and the first thought that comes to our mind is that, they should get a job. If I can work, then so can they. Look upon one successful individual, such as King David, many would love to have had his riches, but so many would not and could not put forth the work effort that he had, in order to achieve as much as he did. A man that is known of great wealth and prosperity over flowing with riches is automat-

ically presumed to be a hard worker with a known record of accomplishment. Think of how many wealthy individuals it is today, one of them could be you. Their actions and efforts has spoken. Your hand personality exhibits the true character that you are. It forms your character of classification, and it speaks for you even when you say nothing. Success and achievement is a photograph of who you have been in your past. No one realistically thinks about where you are going once you reach the top. They only know that now you are an achiever. Your hand does have a personality, it represents your worth to many and it is proof of your working ability. Because many people are noticed for their life's work and it is the work of our hands that motivate others. However, a polite personality with powerful vision will speak forever and ever. Because of their great achievements and good deeds. For they will speak some form of victory. In the way they contribute back into our communities, charities in most cases there's a life-changing message that proves this particular individuul was or is a great successor. That is the message that we all want to send to the ones that can see us, live around us and that are depending on us daily. Surly, the wealthy did

The Anointing Powers Of Your Hands

*not accumulate such form of great wealth by doing noth-
ing, but they has gained greatly in their lives by doing
whatever it took to make it necessary or they inherited it.
John 13:3 says, Jesus knowing that the Father had given
all things into his hands, and that he was come from God,
and went to God. Remember heaven is loaded with your
needs and Jesus has the power to turn things in your life
around.*

*Look upon the movement ability that are
in your hands and think upon the life changing ability that
is right there at your fingertips. After all it is your life,
your vision and your prosperity. David, never looked on
his own ability, but always towards his Fathers ability. He
lifted his hands in the manner that God had lifted them, he
believed not in himself, but David kept his belief fully in
God. First, understand it is the work of your hands that
make the person that you are. Your hands are distinctive;
they bring character towards your personality. If you
realize the manner that others perceive you, it is only
because the way your hands have proven their working
ability through the bringing out of your personality. Many*

view success by what one has in stead of who one is. Honest, truthful, helpful and being pure is an awarded way to describe a great successor. Though money may help your current situation, but a person with a heart of gold is genuine. They can change your way of looking at life. Perhaps, they may give you that extra confidence you need. David proved to the world that God was in him, God created him and that God is all - powerful. A hand personality will show others your success, and your success is your proof that you gained the victory. An individual that is truly tired of their situations, issues and strongholds are going to do something life changing about it. Jesus saw the workload that God had put before Him in the form of an illustration. The work was so mighty, so huge, until He knew that He needed the strength of God to do it in Him. One that is known for an achiever effect is most definitely going to strive for greater, because they are going to change their hand personality. If you are tired of struggles in your life, then you will begin to do something about it by working greater. On the other hand, perhaps you will be ready to begin a new adventure such as your own business, now you are ready to work it. You will think with

The Anointing Powers Of Your Hands

a new mind set being set on the Anointing. In addition, you will move with the works of your hands through the powers of God. Just as Jesus, healed many by the laying on of His hands, He prayed for many by the folding of His hands and He Anointed many by the touch of His hands. You will allow the Spirit of God to begin a magnificent work through the laying on of your hands. Put your hands on I and let The Anointing unravel your prize.

Part Nine

Oops My Hands Fell Into Sin

"Sometimes I don't feel that I am worthy to praise Him."

The Anointing Powers Of Your Hands

God wants you to realize the change, He can do in your life. It will be a powerful effect. Psalms 24:1 says, The EARTH is the LORD's, and the fullness thereof; the world, and they that dwell therein. He has the power right now to turn your life around and make it completely new, but it is up to how bad you want it. He took His time to create so much in this world. God wants you to realize that if He have the power to create a whole world in a manner of days, then most surely He have the power to make your vision come to reality. That is why He gave you the vision, desire it and it shall prosper. Psalms 26:7 says, That I may publish with the voice of thanksgiving, and tell of all thy wondrous works. Allow Him the glory of your work. The sooner you finish, the sooner He will receive the glory.

Though sometimes as you are going through, you may begin to feel the pressures of life. Surely some will influence your mind and give you many reasons to quit, but do not give into them. The majority of the times that is while trouble comes our way, to get us off track.

154

The Anointing Powers Of Your Hands

Psalms 119:66 says,Teach me good judgment and knowledge: for I have believed thy commandments.We must always remember regardless of our circumstance, do good.

I do understand just how you feel especially when you feel all odds are against you. It is hard jumping through the loop holes, especially when you are tired of disappointments. Whenever you are trying to accomplish something greater, you must prepare yourself for victory. Always expect the power of God to send you higher. Remember you are not doing this alone; God has full control over it, so there is no need to worry. Once you are able to overcome, you will know without a shadow of a doubt that you are a born achiever. You may appear to many to be a complete failure at everything you do. Well I am here to tell you that you are a perfect candidate to receive power from The Most High. God loves those that seem to be complete failures, because they are the perfect ones for Him to receive full glory, He exalts them. Failures get the job done, because they are normally a show off for God. Meaning that God will receive greater glory. No one

The Anointing Powers Of Your Hands

in their right mind expects a failure to make it, that is why God receives so much glory as they achieve. Everyone will know it was only God. He has the power to fill up the emptiness. Luke 6:38 says, Give, and it shall be given unto you; good measure, pressed down, and shaken together, and running over, shall men give into your bosom. For with the same measure that ye mete withal it shall be measured to you again. There is more to this scripture than gaining money, you must endeavor in this venture with your all and all. For years you have given to everyone and everything else, now it is time for you to be rewarded. After Jesus work was complete, He received all power and rest. Once you reach your fullness (The finishing of your work), then you will be able to rest and enjoy life. Accomplish things you never thought you could, it will make you feel more complete. God produces fullness to the effect of running over for the ones that believe in Him. Dwell in His word, never run on empty. Just as you may purchase something that is beautiful, you want to be complemented. Well God is the same way, He can take a nobody to make many people notice that He lifted them, until they all will be amazed. Psalms 23:5 says, Thou preparest a table

The Anointing Powers Of Your Hands

before me in the presence of mine enemies: thou anointest my head with oil; my cup runneth over. Look how God took David and then exalted him King. From a child David believed, that his Lord was stronger than him. Exalt Him through the work of your hands. I looked like nothing to many people and for many years, but God was preparing me a greater life in the presence of my enemies. While they was laughing, God was preparing me. Though it may be extremely hard on you, hold out. Surely no one will believe as you can, so therefore continue until it is finish. No one believed that little David was going to beat a Giant less known become one of the greatest Kings. He grew up being a servant and his life was full filled as many has served him.

Most people are caught off track and cannot achieve, because of their own failures. Many have always quoted that if you are not a threat to the enemy, then He is not going to bother you. The enemy does not want the children of God to succeed, because as you succeed you will greatly influence many. Blessed will be your first name and highly favored will be your last.

The Anointing Powers Of Your Hands

Causing the enemy to denounce himself out of your life. The enemy can continue to throw obstacles in your pathway as he thinks will shut down your vision and he can ruin your future. That is why he is trying so hard to get you to quit and give up on your dreams. Whatever you do don't listen to the enemy, but follow the Anointing until you reach your goal. Understand there is a reason for everything, take upon this opportunity to learn from it, but allow it not to break you. I honestly lost count of the many times I fail in life. It took every falling thing in order for me to run for greater and not to fall anymore. However, it took me to fall numerous times to depend greater on the power of God to pick me up. I got tired of falling, so I stood as a statue, firm on the word. I am not speaking on the times, you fall down on purpose. Moreover, the mere accidents and incidents that will cause a powerful move if you are serious. It will cause you to want your path redirected, it will show you the wrong from the right and it will cause God to do something awesome in your lifeProverbs 3:16 says,The length of days are in her right hand; and in her left hand are riches and honor.

The Anointing Powers Of Your Hands

Think upon the days of Adam and Eve, she took her hand to eat of the forbidden fruit, it caused her to fall into sin. Regardless of which hand it was, it was one or the other. Definitely both of your hands have a purpose to serve in the vision that you have. When one begins the work, then the other receives the reward of it. Just as Eve took upon the forbidden fruit, it caused her and Adam to come into a Sinful Nature. Psalms 119:66 says,Teach me good judgment and knowledge: for I have believed thy commandments.We must always remember regardless of our circumstance, do good.You must be careful on what you allow your hands to touch and who's influencing you. Because for everything that they touch there will be a just reward. In addition, you want the right rewards. Titus 3:8 says, This is a faithful saying, and these things I will that thou affirm constantly, that they which have believed in God might be careful to maintain good works. These things are good and profitable unto men.

A hand that falls will have to work harder towards it's goals to achieve. However, understanding the reason why they have fallen in the first place. God wants you to see the glory of the work of your hands, when it is finished what a day of recompense it shall be for you. A day He shall be glorified through your good deeds. Notice the achievements and desire the affects of the rewards. Allow your hands to work diligently. Often times we fail, but in our failures God just wants our eyes to be opened with a broader aspect of what He expects from us. As Eve took part and then initiated the eaten of the forbidden fruit to Adam, they both suffered. We were never created to suffer, hurt or to live under pressure. However, due to sinful nature many will suffer because of who they influence and whose influencing them. God never created us to have to work so hard, He created us to be awesomely blessed, but because of the disobedience, some of us are still born in a cursed generation. Well today, that curse of sinful nature can be broken, but this curse can only be broken through the manor you allow your hands to work towards your achievements. If you were born into a rich family then 95% of the time you will stay rich, but on the other hand if you are born into a family of poverty, then 75% of the times you will live life struggling. That is the true value of being born blessed and just because you have

The Anointing Powers Of Your Hands

already been birthed, does not mean you missed the opportunity of being blessed. If you set in your mind today on the true purpose that God created you and no longer considering your fore fathers, then today God can birth you a whole new life. Every time one fails, it is only because of a minute problem somewhere and all it needs is correcting. A determined person that falls will always get back up. They will not accept their failure as a failure just a scratch and guess what, after time your scratch will disappear. Think if Eve would have just surrounded her present state of thinking ability around, when she ate from the forbidden fruit. Stop analyzing and thinking of your down falls. Once you realize that you were in the wrong or perhaps your hands have touched things that God had forbidden, just ask Him of forgiveness and move on with your life. Just as He sent Adam and Eve forth, God wants to do the same with you. Genesis 3:22 says, And the Lord God said, Behold, the man is become as one of us, to know good and evil: and now, lest he put forth his hand, and take also of the tree of life, and eat, and live for ever.

The Anointing Powers Of Your Hands

One thing you must understand is that God is not at all like man, God is a forgiving God that gives instruction for Life. Adam had to step forward as well as Eve. If they had stayed there, they probably would have gone against God again. There is a strength that is combined in the work of your hands but your eyes must see it until the work of your hands will bring forth proof. You must feel this work with your heart compassion that nothing will ever interfere with it. Now that you understand the only way it will speak, is when you put your hands on it and finish it. Surely tilling your ground is going to be hard work, but it needs your true dedication with a numerous amount of strength capacity. I have learned through life that two hands are better than one. God wants the work of your hands to live and to form your life purpose. He wants it to be brought into realityPsalms 37:24 saysThough he fall, he shall not be utterly cast down: for the Lord upholdeth him with his hand.

I know there are many times when I felt that I was never going to make it through. I felt the spirit of Job every time I felt that I was tormented without a

The Anointing Powers Of Your Hands

cause. I too once was a Job traveling through much travail, but deserving far greater than what I had. Not only was I true to God, but also I had to encounter my patient period of development. Before I had a one on one personal suffering experience with the spirit of Job, going through waiting patiently for my God to deliver me. I just wanted to quit. Just as Job I wondered why? I always had things in my life go accordingly as I had planned them to go. I did not want to adjust to patience, because being patient can be very agonizing, long and it can cause many disappointments. Being patient also made me question my self? I know how you feel. You feel as though things will never go right in your life. You may be feeling just as I felt, what is the use of trying when all you try continues to fail. In addition, every time failure comes it hurts, because you know deep in your heart that everything is going to finally come together. Well do not let the trying times stop you. Psalms 24:1 says, The EARTH is the Lord's, and the fullness thereof; the world, and they that dwell therein. Keep trying regardless how hard things get, how impossible it seems, because "It Ain't What It Looks Like". Once Bishop L. D. Parker preached a beautiful message just as

The Anointing Powers Of Your Hands

I was going through my Job experience, "It Ain't What It Looks Like." It moved me greatly; from that day on, I continued to quote that exact same phrase every time I thought that all else had fail in my life, "It Ain't What It Looks Like." No matter what obstacles came my way trying to tare down my hope, I continued to say, "IT AIN'T WHAT IT LOOKS LIKE". As the next door slammed me in my face and I felt that God was not listening to me. The faith walk I took brought forth no evidence that I was a believer during this critical time in my life. Every time the though came in my mind that I was not going to make it, I thought about that message. This message has carried me from 2001 to the present and it will carry me for the rest of my life. I learned from that one message to look at things not like they appear, but as I wanted them to be. I know what my eyes see, but I believe in my faith and not my sightJohn 14:1 says,LET NOT your heart is troubled: ye believe in God, believe also in me.

You may have being on your face searching for the powers of God and hoping to be delivered. Your situation is tormenting and you wonder if God is hearing you. Surely, we all go through those trials and sometimes they seem to have no end. Despite your efforts, still no end. You have worked so hard to succeed and still it seems to quickly fade away. Almost in the blink of an eye. Surely, it hurts and most definitely it is a hardship. It is over loading your strength capacity, it's eye gripping and tear trenching, but you hold on. Everything you have put your hands to do is dying before your eyes. Every body that you have loved seems to be disappearing from your inner circle, just hold on. God never intended us to be troubled with the cares of this world, that is why we must always keep our focus on the powers of God. Even through times of death of a loved one, God does not expect us to be troubled, but to place all that we have left in the inside of our hearts. The troubles will soon disappear. Proverbs 21:1 says,The King's heart is in the hands of the Lord, as the rivers of the water: he turneth it whithersoever he will.

No matter what Job lost he continued to call upon the name of the Lord, he continued to look up to the hills where his help came from. The majority of things in our life are not recognized as faith seeds. If you

The Anointing Powers Of Your Hands

really ever go through enough you will stop giving in to failure and begin to look at your lost. Expect greater to come in your life, than before. Calculating a major lost and still trusting in the Lord only increase favor from the Lord. Regardless of how awful a situation may appear, I always like to keep my eyes remaining on just one piece of good to come out of it. As an example, hurricane Katrina destroyed buildings, homes, businesses, separated families and friends. However, God had to separate many people in order to change some lives. It also took many lives that could never be replaced. The love ones that did not survive this major storm, caused many to become greater survivors. When God has put out an order for your life, He will do what ever it takes just to get to that one. He knew some praying child believed in Him for a brighter future. And someone asked Him for a miracle, so many received many blessings that set them up for the rest of their lives. Perhaps, some needed to become believers and some had forgot that He was God - while others forgot how to love. Through this mighty devastation, many grew to love one another without showing partiality. Hearts was opened to give love as loved poured out of many hearts. Everyone began to lend a helping hand as we all was devastated because of the storms. People all over the world began to call on God on the behalf of all the victims and lives were forever changed. God will have His way at any measure just to be recognized, God had planned it long before you and I was ever birthed. Many want to put all their focus on the destruction of the storms, but look at all the blessings that came out of Katrina. Some people was blessed with more afterwards than before. Some obtained a debt free home, better developments, and better quality of schools for their children. In addition, some were just disconnected with all the wrong people heading for full destruction. God needed to change some life styles, relationships and redirect some lives. God hands covered so many as they could not look towards the help of the city, state or even federal government. So therefore, they only had to depend on the hand of God. Look at the many people that looked down on the poor, homeless and the less fortunate, but for the rest of their lives they will never look down on them again in the same manner. They will have compassion to love them always being reminded that one day they too were once there. Storms come in all shapes, sizes and they can travel at any force of wind to tare down, abuse, hurt or wound any body's life and it does not matter if we're prepared. When a storm rages through if you are in its pathway, then you too will be caught up well as all that surrounds. Many will fill the effects of the aftermath. However, remember the power is in the storm creator, just as He allows the thunder to roar He can allow *PEACE IN THE STORM. John 14:27says, Peace I leave with you, my peace I give unto you: not as the world giveth, give I unto you. Let not your heart be troubled, neither let it be afraid.*

You will also experience magnificent gratitude, being appreciative for the simple things in life. The things that many have forgotten to show God we appreciate Him. God allows the enemy to tempt His true servants, just to strengthen them. If you can overcome temptation when you are proving to God that you are His. Overcoming temptation will cause you to gain more victory. Temptation is evil but once you gain the interest of overcoming, then you will have a new life perspective.

The Anointing Powers Of Your Hands

Your heart will not be troubled any more through weakness, but greater appreciation will cause you to triumph. Believe greater in the powers of God and heaven will show you things you never thought your eyes would ever see. Just say no to sin and yes to His will.

Part Ten

Finger Out Your Faith

"When you realize which direction God is sending you, then you will go".

The Anointing Powers Of Your Hands

Surely Go has given you a commission. Perhaps more than once you have heard His voice, but now it is time to listen. Moreover, you heard Him as He whispered to you. Many times, you have dreamed of your life being everything you ever hoped for. Then you woke up still stuck in the same predicament day in and day out. Proverbs 3:5 says,Trust in the Lord with all thine heart; and lean not unto thine own understanding Often saying, what if this dream was true? Hoping that you could live that dream. Sometimes feeling that you would be better off if you had never woke up. Surely we all have felt that way one time or another, especially when we cannot handle the pressures of life. Many things have appeared in our lives that we did not expect. Life crisis has thrown you off guard and the way your life appears was nowhere in your life plans. Things happened to you without notice and actually you wished your life was a dream. It seems like you, have been marked to be destroyed. Moreover, none of this was suppose to happen to you, but it did. Nevertheless, still no real proof of your dreams coming to reality. Perhaps, you have tried and you may have tried in many ways. Still

The Anointing Powers Of Your Hands

nothing has seemed to work out. You want a better life but how bad do you desire it. Your hopes soon turn to dreams and your dreams soon turned into a brief moment of happiness, until you wake up. Sometimes your mind has drifted into your dream world, hoping for this dream to come true. Moreover, doubt begins to laugh in your face and surface in your mind, now your dreams are cancelled out. Your hopes are now hopeless and there is no desperation causing you to continue to hope for your dreams to be true. However, you wanted it all to happen, growing up with many great expectations for your life, but your life has seemed to go down the drain. I am here to tell you that you need this vision to work, do not quit hoping for it now. Find some new hope and let your new hope cause your dreams to come true. If God did it for me, He too can do it for you. The key is no matter what has happened in my life, I never stopped visualizing seeing my dreams come to reality. I never gave up and I was not prepared to let anything stop me. Slam on the gas and get off the brakes, let your dreams accelerate. You need it to be real. Let your effort push you forward. Your life destiny is depending on it. You want it and you have tried in every way, but did you

The Anointing Powers Of Your Hands

give it all you had. Did you push yourself into God's Anointing Powers? For when you reach the depths of His powers, then your vision will speak boldly. His Anointing will prosper your vision and increase will flow into operation. I want you to understand this one thing, only you can cause it to come forth. If you do not desire it strong enough, then God does not have to let it happen. Perhaps your dreams were not large enough to cause Him to move on your behalf. However, He intentionally wanted you to believe in Him for a miracle that is going to forever affect the way you think of Him. Dreams are in a world of it's own but reality is what you live in. Let God bring your dreams into reality. No matter how large your dreams are remember God will give you your heart desires. If you desire it, then it is yours. If you believe that He is able, then it is already done and if you know Him, what are you still doing dreaming? God is a God of prosperity and He lives to purposely cause the dead to rise in Him. Get more of God and be enlarged. All you have to do is delight yourself in Him. Psalms 37:4 says, Delight thyself also in the Lord, and he shall give thee the desires of thine heart.

The Anointing Powers Of Your Hands

Just think about all the things that you will be able to do, with the Anointing Powers of God working in you. If you really use what He has blessed you with, then you will receive The Anointing. You will have the power to do anything you set your mind to do. It does not matter how big your dreams are. God has the power to bring them all to reality. It does not matter if you have multiple visions. I mean enough to fill the largest football stadium in the world. It can happen for you. It does not matter if your dreams are great enough to fill a whole city or even the world. That is an example of how large God wants your heart desires to be in Him. Your dreams will only live through the faith that you have in The Powers of God. If you think small, then you will only believe little in Him. Get over that mustard seed of faith and let your faith grow up in Him. God wants to develop your faith, as He will cause it to mature. Allow Him to manifest everything within your life. Let Him give you hope that will cause you to gain more life. As you will gain a greater life and cause many others to survive off your hope. It is time to realize the many life opportunities that will live because of your dreams. God has the power for you to do it all. How many lives can be affected through the reality of your dreams? The work of your hands is going to affect many either to be encouraged or discouraged. Your hands posse's powers, but which powers do they currently posses? Are they affecting lives to desire Jesus more or are they canceling out other's faith? Sometimes our dreams do not come true, because God is not finish showing us the whole dream. Other times, it is because our hearts and minds may not be prepared for all that He has for us. He wants The Power of Love to work through our hands. God wants someone else to be connected to Him through our works. He wants our lives to speak that He is real and to know that He lives. You need spiritual motivation, it is your only possibility for you to achieve all the visions He has given you. The Anointing can do it all. It is just waiting on you. I am one that knows about vision. I too have had many. I had so many my aunt once said to me, "do you think you are trying to do too much at one time." At first, I thought I did, but it was my many dreams that kept me running forward. Apparently I was, but I believed so much in the word of God and I knew He gave them all to me. I was not prepared to put one vision on the back burner. Soon after-

The Anointing Powers Of Your Hands

wards, Jamie Fox appeared on The Oprah show a very gifted man in many ways. He said, "You can do it all." Looking back over his many accomplishments, I realized if he could; then so can I. He is one with many talents and has been a great achiever in many ways. Remember, if someone else can then so can you. Though you think your dreams are too big for you, they are just right for God to bless them to come forth.

Every vision that God has given you is for a purpose, to bring you out in many ways. He wants you to put your hands on it. My visions helped saved my life and I simply needed them all. I begin to work in every angle I could in order to achieve. They all lifted my spirits and kept me motivated in Him. Many times, I wanted to give up but I could not. When God gives you a vision it is made to be spiritual. His Spirit saved my life repeatedly and the many visions caused me to run on. Every song, book, business and vision for the ministry was God's way of giving me new hope. God wants you to hold on and move forward in your life. Things will get better, actually they will be so good you will begin to burst out and just laugh.

The Anointing Powers Of Your Hands

God has a mighty way of making us laugh without anything even being funny. His love is different and it is beyond words I cannot express, it is wonderful. Proverbs 22:6 says, Train up a child in the way he should go: and when He is old, he will not depart from it.

If it was not for the many visions that God had given me, I often wondered where would my children's destiny be? Our children suffer as we do. They too feel the pressures of life. Often time's parents do not realize the agony we put our children through. However, due towards our insecurities, effortless progress to cause a life change and the fear of moving forward deprives our families of many securities. The same way you feel your life is in a mess is the same way our children feel too. Believe me they know when their parent's are stressed out, actually they are smarter than we credit them. God knew I needed my visions, because they kept inspiring me to live. They also gave my children hope and caused them to believe more in Him. I wanted God to know that I appreciated every gift, talent and vision He had given me. I ran with them all, because each vision served its own purpose.

The Anointing Powers Of Your Hands

Know that your dreams serve a purpose not only to give life, but also to save lives. As you will begin to let The Anointing flow through your hands, God will bring your needs forth. As I continued my children were inspired and as they saw me achieve they too begin to gain vision. The Anointing Powers of your hands will simply connect someone else with greater hope. Allow God to work through you, then He will begin to work through your children. As a parent, I wanted to train my children to believe that God is real. I wanted them to carry on in my footsteps as I taught them to fear Him. Simply teaching them the right from the wrong. We must let God Anoint the works of our hands, so that our children can grow up knowing that The Anointing is real. The best way to teach someone is to show him or her the way. Show your children that The Anointing is in you. Teach them to desire The Anointing Powers of God through the way you live. Children live and learn through our lifestyles. What way are you showing your child and which way are you leading them? Whatever you are, they too will become. Teach them that the impossibilities are possible.

The Anointing Powers Of Your Hands

You must know that you are a visionary. A dreamer only has dreams but a visionary reaches their destiny. The Anointing Powers of God will work in you. He wants you to put your hands to work on the vision He has giving you. Only you can desire it in your heart until God will allow it to come forth. Put your hands to work and God will anoint them. He will give you the power and your vision shall speak for it self. Lay your hands on it, as God will surge His Anointing Powers through you.

Genesis 1:27 says So God created man in His own image, in the image of God created he him; male and female created he them. God has given you a perfect hand design. Out of the majority of the jobs, you need to apply your self with hands on training. So many have what it takes and will not use what God has given them. You must allow the precious blood of The Anointing to flow through your fingertips. They will do a wonderful work and many others will notice. Without you putting your hands on it, then what good are your gifts? I know many people with beautiful voices that will sing your socks off, but they rather work a job paying minimum wage.

The Anointing Powers Of Your Hands

Many people have God given gifts, but they will not trust God enough to get them out of poverty. They have sacrificed their future well as their children's future because of their lack of courage. You must be prepared to show the world what you have working on the inside of you. Show them how The Power of God is in you. Let Him perform a marvelous work as you put your hands on it. I know just as God created this earth He was excited about the beauty thereof. He wanted someone to Glorify His works. God created us so that He can be glorified. Let Him be glorified through you. We all notice how powerful God really is after seeing Him work mightily in another. Let The Anointing Powers in your hands show the world how large God is in you. Isaiah 43:7 says, Even everyone that is called by my name: for I have created him for my glory, I have formed him; yea, I have made him. Though you have been through the trying times, it was to enhance your faith. For every sink hole the enemy prepared for you, God is going to cause you to raise higher. Every time someone has hurt me it has caused me to reach more for Jesus. The more I reached for Jesus, the more I was strengthened by the powers of God. Though He said, "He would make my enemies my foot stool". Simply meaning that while the enemies are trying to break you God is going to be making you. When He finish making you - you will be raised higher than them. All that sorrow, they have caused you was to make you climb higher in life and it caused you to step up. God has a mighty way in getting His chosen to triumph in life, His word cannot go void so therefore stand on it.

God has heavenly powers readily to anoint the works of your hands. When you realize the power that is in God, you will know it is available to you too. He created us in His imagine and He created us to be all - powerful. Let Him begin to flourish His anointing powers through you. Let Him grow larger in you. Put no limits on how large God will expand Himself in you. Just note, as He grows larger in you, then He will be magnified through your children. I do not see God begging for nothing and neither should His children. Everything God wants it is instantly done. God does not have a need, what about you? Isaiah 43:19 says, Behold, I will do a new thing; now it shall spring forth; shall ye not know it? I will

The Anointing Powers Of Your Hands

even make a way in the wilderness, and rivers in the desert. Know that The Anointing is real and powerful things will happen once The Anointing surface in you. No matter how rough things in your life will get, God will make a way. Jesus is the way maker. Just as our children reap from our benefits, a child of God reaps from Heaven. Whatever you need, He has it and if you want it, He will give it to you. In order for God to allow the anointing power to be accepted into your life, then surely things of this world must be pointed out of it. Remember you can only serve one God at a time. When you really mean business and you have a vision, something's must change in your life. Get busy in your vision and make God proud. God created you to be powerful, so therefore you need to indulge yourself in Him. His Anointing is purposed for us to receive power and daily we should show Him appreciation. Respect how you represent Him at all times and watch how He will manifest your reward. You have to know the One you love by satisfying Him fully. After all, it is He that posses the powers to get you to your life destiny and without trust - there is noting. Trust Him and you will receive The Anointing. 1 John 2:27 says, But the anointing

The Anointing Powers Of Your Hands

which ye have received of him abideth in you, and ye need not that any many teach you but as the same anointing teacheth you of all things, and is truth, and is no lie, and even as it hath taught you, ye shall abide in him. Without God, then we would not exist. In addition, without His anointing in my life, I would have never received the Anointing Powers of my hands. I thank God for His Anointing, because it has brought forth many beautiful things in my life. The things that God has placed in my heart and the joy that He brings forth will cause you to be filled with daily happiness. Worldly things cannot compare to the peace of His serenity. I can imagine that Thomas pointed out the doubts that were in his heart with his fingers. You must decide if you are going to continue allowing your life to stay this way or if you are going to put forth, reach higher and receive Heavenly Powers. The Anointing will flow through your fingers causing you to surge energy from heaven and it will work mightily through your hands. John 20:27 says, Then saith he to Thomas, Reach hither thy finger, and behold my hands; and reach hither thy hand, and thrust it into my side: and be not faithless, but believing.

The Anointing Powers Of Your Hands

This man name Thomas was also known to many to be "Doubting Thomas" a name that followed Him, because of his times of doubting the truth about Jesus. Moreover, he reached the point of truth by touching Jesus. Thomas was one considered to always doubt until the truth was made known unto Him. Though he had known of God, he was not sure about Jesus. Even being one of the twelve disciples, Thomas believed in absolutely none of his friend's own words. Thomas wanted true clarity. He was one that believed through seeing and touching for him self. No one could tell him any thing. He simply had to see with his own eyes. He did not have faith. That is exactly why the generations today are going astray, because many have raised their children without knowing Jesus. Though many people know God, so they say they have no faith in Jesus. They can believe that God created the world in a few days and caused Noah to build an ark, but they do not accept that JESUS rose up with all power in His hands. Jesus has all the power. He is The Descender.

The Anointing Powers Of Your Hands

I know only one way that many would not take the word of a friend. It is either that you do not know them that well or that you do not trust him or her. Thomas was known as The Doubter. A doubter is an unbeliever and he or she is one, which needs convincing. I concluded that he never truly knew Jesus because he did not trust that He was the Messiah. Once you know Jesus, there is no turning back. No one in his or her right frame of mind would want to be separated from Jesus, because of His greatness. His love is full of compassion and once you taste and see how sweet He is. You will never crave for another to be your God, only Him. Yes, I was a doubter too before I knew Him. However, now that I know Him I could not live without Him. He has changed my life and has given it a new meaning. Living life without Jesus would be impossible to me. Truly touch Him for yourself.

Jeremiah 29:13 says, And ye shall seek me, and find me, when ye shall search for me with all your heart Sometimes we make life more complicated to search for the truth. It is either that we are simply lazy or do not want to do our own research. Often times, we just have the wrong resources. Faith grows as we decide to reach in the manor to stretch our faith. We must put our priorities in order by pleasing Him first.

First, Thomas needed to put His finger through the wounds of Jesus before He would believe. He wanted to know the truth for himself that Jesus was the Messiah. Many criticized Thomas for doubting. Just as people may criticize you today. Do not let it stop you. He had to touch Jesus, because he wanted to feel Him. Most people would have just taken their friend's advice, but not Thomas. Many people are too trusting, they will trust anyone and anything. Many times people told me things, but nothing in my life changed until I reached for Jesus on my own. You have to delight yourself in Him until you press yourself into The Anointing. The presence of Jesus is powerful, but the touch of Him is more powerful. It is Anointing. However, when I begin to reach forth, I touched Him for myself and Jesus changed my life. Once He touch you there will be a true change, you will not be the same individual you use to be. It does not matter, who you are, where you have been in life and what you are not,

The Anointing Powers Of Your Hands

He is a true Life Changer. No yoke, stronghold or even you can stop yourself once The Anointing comes upon you. Thomas never gave in to what anyone said; neither did he care what anyone thought of Him. Often times too many people are quick to run with what they hear vice versa, than what they know. Thomas was smart I must say He wanted to feel Jesus for himself. Thomas was prepared to do what was necessary to find the truth for himself. He did not want to trust any of the disciples. In many similar cases people will allow what they have heard or saw stop their belief. Thomas was one that made sure no one was going to stop him from finding out the truth. Just because some of the other disciples probably were not what he would have expected them to be. They did not stop him from figuring out the truth for himself. Regardless of your feelings towards another that profess the gospel, do not let it stop you. That is the key focus why so many visions are buried today, they let what some one else say, destroy their dreams. I have heard so many people say that is why I do not go to church. All because of what someone else has done. Do not let what others do, think or say stop you. After all, it will only ruin your life. One saying I love to

The Anointing Powers Of Your Hands

say, "if someone wants to play with their life then let them, but I will not play with mine.

John 20:27 says, Then saith he to Thomas, Reach hither thy finger, and behold my hands; and reach hither thy hand, and thrust it into my side: and be not faithless, but believing. Thomas put his fingers through Jesus wounds. It inspired Thomas faith to go deep. Once he touched Jesus, He was a believer. His faith grew through the wounds of Jesus. He touched The Blood and was moved. Thomas was more than just inspired, He felt The Anointing flowing through His fingertips. Once you begin to touch Jesus as you reach forth, you will fill The Almighty presence of God move through you. God wants your hands to reach up to Him. He wants to anoint you and give you Power. Psalms 45:1 says, MY HEART is inditing a good matter: I speak of the things which I have made touching the King: my tongue is the pen of a ready writer. The key to reaching up is that you aim high. Jesus is The Highest of the High. Be ready and willing and The Anointing will be available to you. He wants you to aim for the height of your life. He wants to give you all of your

The Anointing Powers Of Your Hands

heart desires including your dreams. His purpose is to be your God.

Often many do not reach God in the manner He wants us to. You must look up, aim high and feel His Anointing. Stop letting people, and excuses stop you from reaching The Anointing. It is powerful. I was once in a conversation with one of my clients. She said, "It does not take all of that, shouting, jumping and stuff to praise or worship God." To some maybe no, but for me yes it did. No one knows what He has done for me. When I say if it was not for the Lord on my side, I mean every word. Where would I be? You would be amazed at the many things I had to endeavor, so many until I did not have a choice, but to hold on to the Word. The enemy was set out so powerful against me, I was literally stripped of everything. The more I stretch my hands to THEE, is the more my enemies bomb rushed me. Yes I took a good beating, sometimes I fell down, but thank God I rose back up. There is no other that I can depend on like Him, He is my all and all. Once I felt Jesus for myself, I could not sit there as though I felt nothing. He is too powerful and once you "really" feel The Anointing, you will never be the same. I use to go to church as I was sitting on a log and I sat on my blessings. I would hardly clap my hands or stump my feet and my life did not change. I went to church wanting to receive, but often times I did not. When I realized I had to become a partaker in praise, fellowship and worship then I begin to receive a new part of the life He had purposed for me. I do not have time to give God a high sadity praise, for He has been too good to me. If my praise tend to get a little crazy, perhaps it's because He has blessed me crazy. As they say when the praises go up the blessings will come down and I needed them all. I was not a shouter or worshiper I was just a bench warmer. However, when that day came and I stopped sitting I begin to praise. One day I was no longer worried about if my hair would fall or if my heels would curl over, who cares. I went in expecting a miracle and I came out with a bigger reward. God moves as we move and He works as we work. Eventually I realized my praise grew stronger and so did I. My shouts grew louder and so did His voice. The Anointing is too much to sit down on; it will cause you to be moved 11 Samuel 6:14 says, And David danced before the

The Anointing Powers Of Your Hands

Lord with all his might; and David was girded with a linen ephod. When The Anointing is on you there will be no room for doubt. You need the power of God to move in you, on you and to accomplish anything greater than you. David was one that had overcame many war times. He knew exactly what it meant to come out or to need another victory and he also never forgot his previous victories. David did not have time to give the Lord a high sadity praise, but David put his all and all in his praise. When you praise God, this is not to satisfy you, but Him. Dance before the Lord with all your might. I never forgot my first feeling of the Anointing. It immediately consumed everything out of me that caused me to doubt Him ever again. The Anointing is the most powerful presence you could ever feel, it will soothe your soul as it will also completely make you whole.

Thomas fingertip is what stirred up his faith in Jesus. However, as he pushed himself towards the wounds of Jesus. He stretched his hands and inserted them through Jesus wounds. He received the power of The Anointing. He felt sure with his hands that counseled out

The Anointing Powers Of Your Hands

all his doubt. The pressing, the point, the tip of his fingers plunged into The Anointing. Jesus wounds has caused many to be saved, delivered and powered up. Finally, Thomas was able to see with his eyes and feel the precious blood of Jesus flowing through his fingertips. When you feel Jesus, you will know the purpose of His wounds. The tip of your fingers will begin to transpire the powers of God in your life. I love it as I feel my way through because the eye seeing will sometimes miss-lead you. God is a Spirit. We should look for Him to appear to us in a spiritual manner. You cannot see The Spirit, but you will feel Him. However, once The Anointing comes upon you there will be no sitting still. Thomas just wanted to feel the supreme presence of the Lord for himself. As he pushed his finger, Thomas was instantly delivered. The more you press is the sooner you will feel The Anointing. This press is up to how bad you desire a true heart change in your life. Your heart must feel it and you must press towards it. In your press is your reward. Know that God rewards are forever lasting, they will never die. Seek after the things of Heaven and all the powers you will ever need will be granted to you. They will be right there in the palm of your

The Anointing Powers Of Your Hands

hands. If you want it, then push your way through until you press your way into His Anointing. Just remember, there is an appointed time for your vision to speak. It will not speak a minute sooner neither one second later. Allow nothing or no one to hinder your progress, do whatever you need, so that God will speak boldly through your vision. Put your whole heart effort in laying your hands on this vision that God has given you. Your future is in your press and The Anointing is waiting on your push.

The End of Your Postponed Vision

The Anointing Powers Of Your Hands

Remember your action to move towards Him causes Him to respond to you.

<u>Vision Preparation: 1</u>

Vision is something that takes time and plenty of preparation. The greater effort you put in preparing your vision is the sooner it will come to pass. Write a strong vision and do not rush it. Do all your necessary foot work and research. Plan it out to the tee. It took me years to write my visions. Use every resource you can and then get to know your vision. Visions are personal because they come from within the heart. The more you prepare it, the sooner you will want it and the more your heart is going to desire it. After you have fully prepared your vision, now it is time to make any changes.

<u>Revising Your Vision: 2</u>

Revise it, which simply means you are now proofing it. As you make changes, begin studying your vision. It needs to be fully together. Place it in front of you and keep it at your fingertips. Do not depend on no one to help you, other than God. Add your vision to your meditation and fast over your vision well as pray and allow God to consecrate

The Anointing Powers Of Your Hands

it. God has the power to raise anything up from the dead. He will give your vision life and it will speak.

Do Not Rush Your Vision: 3

There is an appointed time for your vision to speak. It will not speak any sooner, regardless of you trying to rush it. Be patient as God begins to prepare you to handle receiving it. He works at His paste and not yours. Daily continue in these quick notes, keep putting your hands on it. God is going to anoint the work of your hands. Get ready to face the TRUTH for the victory is in your effort.

- *Write down the blessings you want to give.*
- *Write down how your vision is going to please God.*
- *Write down how much you have progressed.*
- *Keep a to do list for your vision, making the steps.*
- *Know the purpose of your vision.*
- *Bless in seven ways within the next 30 days.*
- *Though God has given you the vision, dedicate it back to Him.*

The Anointing Powers Of Your Hands

The Purpose of your vision: 4

It should be to bless someone with love, giving from your heart and helping another. Often times we do not receive our blessings, because our hearts are not where God would have them to be. Many people just do not know how to show love. Prove to God that you have a good heart and start practicing by living it. The more you begin to be a blessing the sooner God is going to bless you. Begin sowing goodness and needed blessings to other people. Listen to their needs and let God lead you to be a blessing to them. Be prepared for more doors to open on your behalf. When we bless with love God blesses us. Perhaps buy someone flowers that are not expecting it. Treat someone to dinner that needs to go somewhere. Buy someone a gift card and mail it to him or her. However, as God blesses you to be a blessing, then you will receive more. Treat a friend to a new outfit, just because. So many wait until Christmas to give gifts, but it should be a year round thing. God wants us to be more of a blessing, spread love, joy and cause someone to want to smile. Do from your heart and watch God work. Hold no grudges in your

The Anointing Powers Of Your Hands

heart, just let it be filled with love. Watch Him work more in your life. If you sow more love, you will receive greater love. Plant seeds of love in many ways, praying for 100 fold return. I tell many to sow what you need and let God increase you. We all want to be loved, after all God is love. So therefore, the purpose of your vision must be in your heart. Follow it and let God lead you into a life you have only dreamed of.

The Anointing Powers Of Your Hands

A vote of thanks: JESUS

First, I give exceedingly great honor to my Heavenly Father -The Most High. I am grateful and it is a privilege to be used by God in any way. LORD I thank you for electing a wretch as I, you looked low and saw me. You touched me and then delivered me. I thank you Lord with everything that is within in me. Lord you are my all and all.

Friends & family:
To all that prayed for me, kept me inspired when I was tired in my spirit and spoke the word of life to keep me encouraged in Him, my heart says thank you deep from within.

I love you all & be richly Blessed.

The Anointing Powers Of Your Hands

Parice Parker

Website: www.booksfolph.com

From my heart to yours as The Holy Spirit speaks through my heart. I can only give the readers that God has designed for me, whatever He allows. I was born to minister in many ways to richly inspire. As you will begin to reach for the impossible, aim for greater and excel in life. I pray in JESUS name that these awesome books, will be a part of your testimony as you triumph with victory.

Inspirational Speaking Engagements

Attention: Parice Parker

P. O. B. 680475 Charlotte, N. C. 28216

Email: parice@booksfolph.com

The Anointing Powers Of Your Hands

Title: Living Life In A
Messed Up Situation 1
ISBN 0-9787162-0-5
$9.99
104 pages

     This book is for those that are going through hell, coming out of hell or either has went through hell. It is Anointed!
     D. W. Moore 111

     It is for the complexed individual, Living Life In A Messed Up Situation Volume One. It will teach those that are Living Life In A Messed Up Situation to continue their hope, even when their hope has walked out on them. It is one of the smallest books of 2007 packed with pure power for you to simply gain it all.

The Anointing Powers Of Your Hands

A Series Packed With Pure Power

Living Life In A
Messed Up Situation
Volume Two

Are U Fishing For Your Miracle?
"Let Jesus Catch U Trying"

Parice Parker

Title: Living Life In A Messed
Up Situation Volume 2

ISBN 0-978-7162-2-1

170 Pages

$13.95

This inspirational novel will inspire you to show God something out of your nothing. Impress Jesus with your trying ability and

"Let Jesus Catch U Trying".

Living Life In A Messed Up Situation - Volume 2

Fountain of Life Publisher's House